JELL-O® BRAND

fun and fabulous recipes

JELL-O® BRAND

fun and fabulous recipes

from
JELL-O®
Gelatins & Puddings

BEEKMAN HOUSE

© 1988 General Foods Corporation

Angel Flake, Baker's, Birds Eye, Cool Whip, Dream Whip, German's, Jell-O,
Maxwell House and Yuban are registered trademarks of General Foods Corporation,
White Plains, NY 10625.

On the front cover: Gelatin Trifle *(see page 22).*

On the back cover, clockwise from top left: Fruit Whip *(see page 79),*
Chocolate Turtle Pie *(see page 17),* Ginger Pineapple Mold *(see page 61),*
Cherry-Topped Icebox Cake *(see page 163).*

Library of Congress Catalog Card Number: 87-63421

ISBN: 0-517-65521-7

This edition published by:
Beekman House
Distributed by Crown Publishers, Inc.
225 Park Avenue South
New York, New York 10003

Printed and bound in Yugoslavia by Zrinski

h g f e d c b a

CONTENTS

JELL-O® DESSERT PERFECTION

For ideal results with JELL-O® Brand Gelatin and JELL-O® Pudding and Pie Filling, follow the preparation tips, general hints and serving ideas given in this section. To start, always follow basic package or recipe directions. Then use these tips to make truly perfect creations!

Self-Layering Dessert (see page 91)

Gelatin Tips

To make a mixture that is clear and uniformly set, be sure the gelatin is *completely* dissolved in boiling water or other boiling liquid before adding the cold liquid.

JELL-O Brand Gelatin and Sugar Free Gelatin can be used interchangeably in recipes.

To double a recipe, simply double the amounts of gelatin, liquid and other ingredients used, except salt, vinegar and lemon juice. For these ingredients, use just 1½ times the amount given in the recipe.

To store prepared gelatin overnight or longer, cover it to prevent drying. Always store gelatin cakes or pies in the refrigerator.

IN A HURRY

Speed up the chilling time by choosing the right containers or using one of these specially developed speed-set methods.

The container: Use metal bowls or molds rather than glass, plastic or china. Metal chills more quickly and the gelatin will be firm in less time than in glass or plastic bowls. Individual servings in small molds or serving dishes will also chill more quickly than large servings.

The ice cube method: Completely dissolve gelatin in ¾ cup boiling liquid (1½ cups for 8-serving size package). Combine ½ cup cold water with ice cubes to make 1¼ cups ice and water (1 cup cold water and ice cubes to make 2½ cups for 8-serving size package). Add to gelatin, stirring until slightly thickened. Remove any unmelted ice. Pour into dessert dishes or bowl. Chill. Soft-set and ready to eat in about 30 minutes. *Do not* use this method if you are going to mold the gelatin.

The blender method: Place 4-serving size package of gelatin and ¾ cup boiling liquid in blender. The volume of an 8-serving size package is too large for most blenders. Cover and blend at low speed until gelatin is completely dissolved, 30 seconds. Combine ½ cup cold water and ice cubes to make 1¼ cups; add to gelatin. Stir until partially melted. Blend at high speed 30 seconds. Pour into dessert dishes or bowl. Chill until set, at least 30 minutes.

The ice bath method: Dissolve gelatin according to package directions. Then place the bowl of gelatin mixture in another bowl of ice and water; stir occasionally as mixture chills to ensure even thickening.

MICROWAVE WAY

Prepare gelatin in your microwave oven following these easy directions.

The microwave method: Pour 1 cup water into 1-quart microwave-safe bowl or 2-cup measure (2 cups water, 1½-quart bowl or 4-cup measure for 8-serving size). Add gelatin. *Do not stir.* Heat, uncovered, at HIGH, about 2 to 2½ minutes (3 to 3½ minutes for 8-serving size), until gelatin is dissolved. Add 1 cup cold water (2 cups for 8-serving size). Chill until set.

Or, bring water to a boil at HIGH, about 2 minutes (3 minutes for 8-serving size). Pour over gelatin in bowl; stir until dissolved. *Do not add gelatin to boiling water.*

Microwave speed-set method: Pour ¾ cup water into 1-quart microwave-safe bowl (1½ cups water into 1½-quart bowl for 8-serving size). Add gelatin. *Do not stir.* Heat, uncovered, at HIGH power, about 2½ minutes (3½ minutes for 8-serving size), until gelatin is completely dissolved. Stir. Combine ½ cup cold water and ice cubes to make 1¼ cups ice and water (1 cup cold water and ice cubes to make 2½ cups for 8-serving size). Remove any unmelted ice. Pour into dessert dishes or bowl. Chill until soft-set and ready to eat, at least 30 minutes, or until firm, 1 to 1½ hours.

THE EXTRAS

Add a special touch to your gelatin dessert or salad. Try one of these ideas.

Fruits and vegetables: Chill gelatin until it is thickened, then fold in ¾ to 1½ cups (1½ to 3 cups for 8-serving size) of fruits or vegetables. If gelatin is not thick enough, the fruits or vegetables may float or sink. Do not use fresh or frozen pineapple or kiwifruit or fresh ginger root, papaya, figs or guava. An enzyme in these fruits will prevent the gelatin from setting. These fruits are fine, however, if cooked or canned, because these processes deactivate the enzyme. Canned or fresh fruits should be drained well before adding (unless a recipe specifies otherwise). Fruit juice or syrup can be used as part of liquid called for in the recipes.

Carbonated soft drinks: Substitute carbonated soft drinks, such as cola, ginger ale, root beer or lemon- or lime-flavored mixes, for part or all of the cold water.

Fruit juice: Use fruit juice for part of the liquid—orange juice, apple juice, cranberry juice, tomato juice or canned pineapple juice. Use boiling fruit juice if replacing boiling water.

Flavoring extracts: Add flavoring extracts, such as vanilla, almond, peppermint or rum—just a touch for a flavor plus.

Wine or liqueur: Add a little wine or liqueur for a festive touch. Use 2 tablespoons of white wine, red wine, sherry or port or 1 tablespoon of creme de menthe or fruit-flavored liqueur. For an 8-serving size package, use 3 tablespoons of wine or 1½ tablespoons of liqueur.

Two gelatin flavors: Mix 2 JELL-O Brand Gelatin Flavors for a new flavor combination. Use lemon or orange with any red flavor or combine any 2 red flavors.

QUICK TRICKS

No need to settle for gelatin in the same form every time. Try these different and easy ways with JELL-O Brand Gelatin!

Whip it: Chill prepared gelatin until very thick. Then beat with rotary beater or electric mixer at medium speed until mixture is fluffy and thick and about doubled in volume. Chill until firm. To shorten the chilling time, chill gelatin until slightly thickened, then use ice bath method (see page 8) and beat in bowl set in bowl of ice and water.

Flake it: Prepare gelatin as usual, reducing cold water to ¾ cup (1½ cups for 8-serving size). Pour into shallow pan and chill until firm, about 4 hours. Break into small flakes with fork, or force through ricer or large-mesh strainer. Pile lightly in dishes, alone or with fruit or topping.

Scallop it: Prepare gelatin as usual and pour into sherbet glasses. Chill until firm. Use ½-teaspoon measure to scoop out spoonfuls around edges, making scalloped borders. Top with whipped topping, filling scallops. Use scooped-out gelatin for garnish, if desired.

Cube it: Prepare gelatin as usual, reducing cold water to ¾ cup (1½ cups for 8-serving size). Pour into shallow pan and chill until firm, about 4 hours. Cut in cubes, using sharp knife that has been dipped into hot water. To remove cubes from pan, apply warm wet cloth to bottom of pan, then remove cubes with spatula. Or quickly dip pan in warm water and invert onto plastic wrap. Serve in glasses with cream or fruit, if desired.

Make cutouts: Prepare gelatin as usual, reducing cold water to ½ cup (1 cup for 8-serving size). Pour into 13×9-inch pan (two 13×9-inch pans for 8-serving size) or to ¼-inch depth in other shallow pans. Chill until firm. Cut designs, using cookie cutters that have been dipped in hot water. Transfer cutouts to top of desserts or cakes, using a broad spatula dipped in warm water. If only a few cutouts are needed, flake remaining gelatin with a fork.

Layer it: Make layers with different flavors or different types of gelatin mixtures. Chill each layer until set, but not firm, before adding the next layer. If the first layer is too firm, the layers may slip apart when unmolded. Except for the first layer, the gelatin mixtures should be cool and slightly thickened before being poured into a mold; a warm mixture could soften the layer beneath it and cause mixtures to run together.

Tilt it: This is an unusual way of layering different flavors of mixtures. Prepare gelatin as usual. Fill small stemmed parfait, wine or sherbet glasses about half full. Tilt glasses in refrigerator by catching bases of glasses between bars of the refrigerator rack and leaning tops of glasses against wall. If your refrigerator does not have wire racks, place parfait glasses in a loaf pan and lean tops of glasses against wall. Chill until set, but not firm, then add second mixture. Stand glasses upright and chill until firm.

MOLDING HOW-TOS

Gelatin desserts and salads look their most spectacular when molded. The making and the unmolding can be simple, if you follow these molding tips.

Water: Use less water when preparing the gelatin mixture if dessert or salad is to be molded. For 4-serving size package of gelatin, use ¾ cup cold water. For 8-serving size package of gelatin use 1½ cups cold water. (This adjustment has already been made in recipes in this book that are to be molded.) This makes the mold less fragile and makes unmolding much simpler.

GELATIN TIPS

The mold: Although the decoratively shaped mold is traditional, almost any metal form will work. You can use one of these pans or dishes commonly found in the home: cake pans (8- or 9-inch square or round pans), tube pans (fluted or plain), or loaf pans. Use metal mixing bowls; the nested sets give you a variety of sizes. Or use metal fruit or juice cans; to unmold, dip can in warm water, then puncture bottom of can and unmold.

Size of the mold: Determine the volume of the mold first by measuring with water. Most recipes give an indication of the size of mold needed. For clear gelatin, use a 2-cup mold for a 4-serving size package of gelatin and a 4-cup mold for an 8-serving size package of gelatin. If the mold is smaller than needed, pour the extra gelatin mixture into a separate dish and serve at another time. Do not use a mold that is too large, since it would be difficult to unmold. Either the recipe should be increased or a smaller mold should be used.

Fruits and vegetables: To arrange fruits or vegetables in molds, chill gelatin until thick, then pour about ¼ inch into mold. Arrange fruits or vegetables in a decorative pattern in gelatin. Chill until set, but not firm, then pour remaining thickened gelatin over pattern in mold.

Unmolding: First, allow gelatin to set until firm, several hours or overnight. Also, chill serving plate or individual plates on which mold will be served.

Make certain that gelatin is completely firm. It should not feel sticky on top and should not sag toward the side if mold is tilted.

Use a small pointed knife dipped in warm water to loosen top edge. Or, moisten tips of fingers and gently pull gelatin from edge of mold.

Dip mold in warm, not hot, water, just to the rim, for about 10 seconds. Lift from water, hold upright and shake slightly to loosen gelatin. Or, gently pull gelatin from edge of mold.

Use a chilled serving plate moistened with cold water; this allows gelatin to be moved after unmolding. Place moistened plate over mold and invert. Shake slightly, then lift off mold carefully. If gelatin doesn't release easily, dip the mold in warm water again for a few seconds. If necessary, move gelatin to center of serving plate.

GELATIN CHILLING TIME CHART

In all recipes, for best results, the gelatin needs to be chilled to the proper consistency. Use this chart as a guideline to determine the desired consistency and the approximate chilling time.

When recipe says:	It means gelatin should . . .	It will take about:		Use it for . . .
		Regular set	Speed set*	
"Chill until syrupy"	be consistency of thick syrup	1 hour	3 minutes	glaze for pies, fruits
"Chill until slightly thickened"	be consistency of unbeaten egg whites	1¼ hours	5 to 6 minutes	adding creamy ingredients such as whipped topping, or when mixture will be beaten
"Chill until thickened"	be thick enough so that spoon drawn through it leaves a definite impression	1½ hours	5 to 6 minutes	adding solid ingredients such as fruits or vegetables
"Chill until set but not firm"	stick to the finger when touched and should mound or move to the side when bowl or mold is tilted	2 hours	30 minutes	layering gelatin mixtures
"Chill until firm"	not stick to finger when touched and not mound or move when mold is tilted	individual molds: at least 3 hours 2- to 6-cup mold: at least 4 hours 8- to 12-cup mold: at least 5 hours or overnight	1 hour 2 hours	unmolding and serving

*Ice cube method not recommended for molding.

— ■ —

— ■ —

PUDDING TIPS

The recipes in this book use both JELL-O Pudding and Pie Filling and JELL-O Instant Pudding and Pie Filling. These products are not interchangeable in the recipes. Be sure to use the product called for in the recipe.

JELL-O Sugar Free Pudding and Pie Filling and JELL-O Sugar Free Instant Pudding and Pie Filling can be substituted for their respective cooked and instant pudding mixes.

Although most recipes call for whole milk, you can substitute skim milk, reconstituted nonfat dry milk, light cream or half and half for the whole milk.

Always store prepared pudding desserts and snacks in the refrigerator.

COOKED PUDDING AND PIE FILLING

Stir mixture as it cooks. Bring mixture to a full boil.

For pie filling, cool cooked pudding 5 minutes, stirring twice. Pour into cooled, baked 8-inch pie shell (9-inch highly fluted or 10-inch pie shell for 6-serving size package). Chill 3 hours.

To prepare in the microwave, gradually stir milk into pudding mix in 1½-quart (2-quart for 6-serving size package) microwave-safe bowl. Cook at HIGH for 6 minutes (8 minutes for 6-serving size package) or until mixture comes to a boil, stirring well every 2 minutes. After mixture boils, stir, then chill. For pie filling, cool mixture 5 minutes, stirring twice. Pour into pie shell and chill 3 hours. Note: Ovens vary. Cooking times are approximate. This method is not recommended for ovens below 500 watts.

Pudding will thicken as it cools.

To avoid having a film on the cooled, cooked pudding, cover surface of hot pudding with plastic wrap, placing directly on pudding and pressing down to seal out air.

For a creamier pudding, stir before serving.

— ■ —

INSTANT PUDDING AND PIE FILLING

Always start with *cold* milk. Beat pudding mix slowly, not vigorously.

To prepare by the mixing method, pour cold milk into bowl. Add the mix. With a wire whisk, rotary beater or electric mixer at the lowest speed, beat until well blended, 1 to 2 minutes. Pour into dessert dishes or bowl. For a pie, beat only 1 minute. Mixture will be thin. Pour at once into cooled, baked 8-inch pie shell (9-inch pie shell for 6-serving size package). Chill 1 hour.

To prepare by the blender method, pour cold milk into blender. Add pudding mix. Cover and blend at high speed for 15 seconds. Pour at once into dessert dishes or bowl.

To prepare by the shaker method, pour cold milk into a leakproof 1-quart container (1½-quart container for 6-serving size). Add pudding mix. Cover tightly; shake vigorously for 45 seconds. Pour at once into dessert dishes or bowl. Pudding will be soft-set and ready to eat in 5 minutes. For pie, pour at once into cooled, baked 8-inch pie shell (9-inch pie shell for 6-serving size package). Chill 1 hour.

To prepare JELL-O Instant Pudding and Pie Filling by the fork-stir method, gradually stir milk into pudding mix in 1-quart bowl (1½-quart bowl for 6-serving size package) and continue stirring until blended and smooth, about 2 minutes. Pour at once into dessert dishes or serving bowl. Pudding will be soft-set and ready to eat in 5 minutes.

Glazed Fruit Pie (see page 158)

FAMILY FAVORITES

Win rave reviews when you serve these sensational time-tested treasures. Then get ready to serve them again, as they are sure to become instant traditions and favorites in your own family.

Chocolate Turtle Pie

— ■ —

CHOCOLATE TURTLE PIE

Makes one 8- or 9-inch pie

¼ cup caramel- or butterscotch-flavored dessert topping
1 baked 8- or 9-inch pie shell, cooled
¾ cup pecan halves
1 package (4-serving size) JELL-O® Chocolate Flavor
  Pudding and Pie Filling
1¾ cups milk
1¾ cups thawed COOL WHIP® Non-Dairy Whipped Topping

Place caramel topping in small saucepan. Heat over medium heat until topping comes to a boil, stirring constantly. Pour into pie shell. Arrange pecans on topping and chill.

Combine pie filling mix and milk in medium saucepan; blend well. Cook and stir over medium heat until mixture comes to a full boil. Cool 5 minutes, stirring twice. Pour over nuts in pie shell. Cover surface with plastic wrap. Chill about 3 hours. Remove plastic wrap. Pipe whipped topping around edge of pie. Drizzle with additional topping and garnish with additional pecans, if desired.

GOLDEN SALAD

Makes about 3 cups or 6 servings

1 package (4-serving size) JELL-O® Brand Lemon or
  Orange Flavor Gelatin
½ teaspoon salt
1¼ cups boiling water
1 can (8¼ ounces) crushed pineapple in juice
1 tablespoon lemon juice or vinegar
1½ cups shredded carrots
⅓ cup chopped pecans

Dissolve gelatin and salt in boiling water. Stir in undrained pineapple and lemon juice. Chill until thickened. Stir in carrots and nuts and pour into individual molds. Chill until firm, about 3 hours. Unmold. Serve with crisp salad greens and mayonnaise, if desired.

— ■ —

OLD-FASHIONED BREAD PUDDING

Makes about 4 cups or 6 servings

1 package (4-serving size) JELL-O® Vanilla Flavor Pudding
  and Pie Filling
¼ cup sugar
3 cups milk
¼ cup raisins
2 tablespoons grated lemon rind (optional)
1 tablespoon butter or margarine
½ teaspoon vanilla
6 slices dry white bread, cut into cubes
¼ teaspoon cinnamon
⅛ teaspoon nutmeg

Combine pudding mix and 2 tablespoons of the sugar in medium saucepan. Add 2 cups of the milk; blend well. Add raisins and lemon rind. Cook and stir over medium heat until mixture comes to a full boil. Remove from heat; stir in butter and vanilla.

Pour remaining milk over bread cubes in bowl to moisten; then stir into pudding mixture. Pour into 1-quart baking dish. Combine remaining sugar with spices. Sprinkle over pudding. Broil until sugar is lightly browned and bubbly, 4 to 5 minutes. Serve warm or chilled. Garnish with lemon slice, if desired.

SOUTHERN BANANA PUDDING

Makes 12 servings

1 package (6-serving size) JELL-O® Vanilla or Banana
  Cream Flavor Pudding and Pie Filling
3¾ cups milk
3 eggs, separated
2½ dozen vanilla wafers
2 large bananas, sliced
  Dash salt
⅓ cup sugar

CONTINUED

—■—

Combine pudding mix, milk and egg yolks in medium saucepan; blend well. Cook and stir over medium heat until mixture comes to a full boil; set aside.

Arrange layer of vanilla wafers in bottom of 2-quart baking dish. Place a layer of banana slices over wafers in dish. Spoon a layer of pudding over bananas. Continue layering wafers, bananas and pudding, ending with pudding.

With electric mixer at medium speed, beat egg whites with salt until foamy. Gradually beat in sugar. Beat at high speed until mixture forms stiff shiny peaks. Lightly pile meringue on pudding, sealing edges well. Bake in preheated 425° oven for 5 to 10 minutes or until meringue is lightly browned. Serve warm or chilled.

Clockwise from top left: Southern Banana Pudding, Fruit Crisp (see page 20), Old-Fashioned Bread Pudding

— ■ —

FRUIT CRISP

Makes about 3¼ cups or 6 servings

5 slices white bread
¼ cup butter or margarine
2 tablespoons sugar
1 can (16 to 17 ounces) sliced peaches or fruit cocktail
1 package (4-serving size) JELL-O® Lemon Flavor Instant
   Pudding and Pie Filling
⅛ teaspoon cinnamon
⅛ teaspoon nutmeg
1 cup water

Toast bread and cut into ½-inch cubes. Melt butter in large skillet over medium heat. Add bread cubes and sugar. Cook and stir over medium heat until bread is evenly browned and butter mixture is absorbed; set aside.

Drain fruit, reserving ⅓ cup of the syrup. Blend pudding mix with spices in bowl. Add water and reserved syrup. Stir or beat until mixture is well blended and starts to thicken, about 1 minute; stir in fruit. Pour into serving bowl or individual dessert dishes. Top with bread cubes. Sprinkle with confectioners sugar, if desired. Let stand 15 minutes before serving.

GERMAN SWEET CHOCOLATE PIE

Makes one 9-inch pie

1 unbaked 9-inch pie shell
⅓ cup butter or margarine
⅓ cup packed brown sugar
⅓ cup chopped pecans
⅓ cup BAKER'S® ANGEL FLAKE® Coconut
1 package (6-serving size) JELL-O® Vanilla Flavor Pudding
   and Pie Filling
1 package (4 ounces) BAKER'S® GERMAN'S® Sweet
   Chocolate, broken in pieces
2½ cups milk
1 cup thawed COOL WHIP® Non-Dairy Whipped Topping

CONTINUED

— ■ —

Prick pie shell thoroughly with fork. Bake in preheated 425° oven for 5 to 8 minutes or until shell begins to brown. Remove from oven.

Meanwhile, combine butter, brown sugar, nuts and coconut in medium saucepan. Heat over medium heat until butter and sugar are melted, stirring occasionally. Spread in bottom of hot pie shell. Return to 425° oven for 5 minutes or until bubbly; cool.

Combine pie filling mix, chocolate and milk in medium saucepan. Cook and stir over medium heat until mixture comes to a full boil. Remove from heat and beat to blend, if necessary. Cool 5 minutes, stirring twice. Pour over coconut mixture in pie shell. Cover surface with plastic wrap. Chill about 4 hours. Before serving, remove plastic wrap. Garnish with whipped topping and sprinkle with additional coconut, if desired.

BASIC BAVARIAN

Makes about 3½ cups or 6 servings

1 package (4-serving size) JELL-O® Brand Gelatin, any
  flavor
1 cup boiling water
1 cup cold water
2 cups thawed COOL WHIP® Non-Dairy Whipped Topping

Dissolve gelatin in boiling water. Add cold water. Chill until slightly thickened. Fold in 1½ cups of the whipped topping. Spoon into dessert glasses or 4-cup mold. Chill until firm, about 4 hours. (Unmold, if necessary.) Garnish with remaining whipped topping and fresh or canned fruit, if desired.

Fruit Juice Bavarian: Prepare Basic Bavarian as directed, substituting 1 cup fruit juice for the cold water.

Fruited Bavarian: Prepare Basic Bavarian as directed, adding 1 cup sliced fresh fruit (except pineapple, kiwifruit, mango, papaya or figs).

Bavarian Pie: Prepare Basic Bavarian, Fruit Juice Bavarian or Fruited Bavarian as directed; spoon into cooled baked 9-inch pie shell or graham cracker crumb crust.

—■—

RICHELIEU MOLD

Makes 3½ cups or 6 to 8 servings

¼ cup blanched almonds
1 can (16 ounces) pitted dark sweet cherries
1 package (4-serving size) JELL-O® Brand Gelatin, any red flavor
1 cup boiling water
2 tablespoons orange juice
¾ cup diced orange sections, well drained
1 cup thawed COOL WHIP® Non-Dairy Whipped Topping

Toast almonds in shallow pan in preheated 350° oven for 3 to 5 minutes, stirring once. Chop almonds; set aside. Drain cherries, reserving ⅔ cup of the syrup. Dissolve gelatin in boiling water. Add reserved syrup and orange juice. Chill until slightly thickened. Fold in cherries and oranges. Pour into 4-cup mold or individual molds. Chill until firm, about 4 hours. Combine whipped topping and toasted nuts. Unmold gelatin and serve with topping.

GELATIN TRIFLE

Makes 5½ cups or 10 servings

1 package (4-serving size) JELL-O® Brand Strawberry Flavor Gelatin
¾ cup boiling water
½ cup cold water
   Ice cubes
1 cup sliced strawberries
1 cup sliced bananas
2 cups ½-inch pound cake cubes
¼ cup orange juice
1½ cups cold milk
1 package (4-serving size) JELL-O® Vanilla Flavor Instant Pudding and Pie Filling
½ cup thawed COOL WHIP® Non-Dairy Whipped Topping

CONTINUED

—■—

Completely dissolve gelatin in boiling water. Combine cold water and ice cubes to make 1¼ cups. Add to gelatin, stirring until slightly thickened. Remove any unmelted ice. Stir in strawberries and bananas. Place cake cubes in large serving bowl; sprinkle with orange juice. Spoon gelatin mixture over cake in bowl. Chill 10 to 15 minutes.

Meanwhile, pour cold milk into mixing bowl. Add pudding mix. With electric mixer at low speed, beat until well blended, 1 to 2 minutes. Let stand a few minutes to thicken. Fold in whipped topping. Spoon over gelatin in bowl. Chill. Garnish with additional whipped topping, strawberry slices and banana slices brushed with lemon juice, if desired.

QUICK APPLE PIE

Makes one 9-inch pie

1 can (20 ounces) apple slices, undrained

½ cup water

1 package (4-serving size) JELL-O® Vanilla Flavor Instant
    Pudding and Pie Filling

½ teaspoon cinnamon

¼ teaspoon nutmeg

1 baked 9-inch pie shell, cooled

½ cup graham cracker crumbs

1 tablespoon sugar

2 tablespoons butter or margarine, melted

CONTINUED

Combine apples, water, pie filling mix and spices in medium bowl. Stir until thoroughly blended. Spoon into pie shell. Combine crumbs, sugar and butter; mix well. Sprinkle over pie filling in pie shell. Let stand 1 hour at room temperature before serving.

Note: To serve warm, let stand 1 hour at room temperature; then heat in preheated 350° oven for 10 to 15 minutes.

GELATIN HEAVENLY HASH

Makes 4 cups or 8 servings

1 package (4-serving size) JELL-O® Brand Gelatin, any
    flavor
¾ cup boiling water
½ cup cold water
    Ice cubes
1 cup thawed COOL WHIP® Non-Dairy Whipped Topping or
    sour cream
1 can (20 ounces) crushed pineapple, drained
1 can (11 ounces) mandarin orange sections, drained
1 cup miniature marshmallows
¼ cup chopped walnuts or pecans

Completely dissolve gelatin in boiling water. Combine cold water and ice cubes to make 1¼ cups. Add to gelatin, stirring until slightly thickened. Remove any unmelted ice. Add whipped topping, blending until smooth. Stir in pineapple, mandarin oranges, marshmallows and nuts. Pour into serving bowl or individual dessert dishes. Chill until set, about 2 hours. Garnish with additional fruits and mint leaves, if desired.

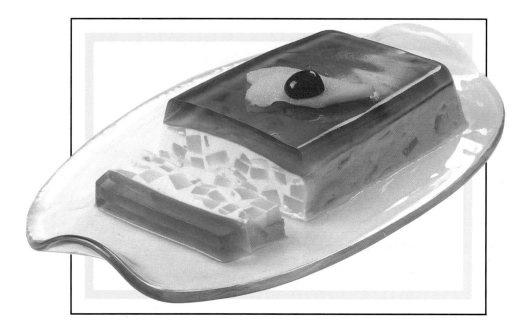

UNDER-THE-SEA SALAD

Makes about 3½ cups or 6 servings

- 1 can (16 ounces) pear halves in syrup
- 1 package (4-serving size) JELL-O® Brand Lime Flavor Gelatin
- ¼ teaspoon salt (optional)
- 1 cup boiling water
- 1 tablespoon lemon juice
- 2 packages (3 ounces each) cream cheese, softened
- ⅛ teaspoon cinnamon (optional)

Drain pears, reserving ¾ cup of the syrup. Dice pears; set aside. Dissolve gelatin and salt in boiling water. Add reserved syrup and lemon juice. Measure 1¼ cups of the gelatin; pour into 8×4-inch loaf pan or 4-cup mold. Chill until set but not firm, about 1 hour.

Very slowly blend remaining gelatin into cream cheese, beating until smooth. Add cinnamon and pears; spoon over clear gelatin in pan. Chill until firm, about 4 hours. Unmold. Garnish with additional pears and maraschino cherry, if desired.

— ■ —

BANANA LAYERED PIE

Makes one 9-inch pie

2¼ cups cold milk
1 package (6-serving size) JELL-O® Vanilla Flavor Instant
   Pudding and Pie Filling
1 baked 9-inch pie shell or prepared graham cracker crumb
   crust, cooled
2 medium bananas
½ cup thawed COOL WHIP® Non-Dairy Whipped Topping
   Lemon juice

Pour cold milk into bowl. Add pie filling mix. With electric mixer at low speed, beat until blended, about 1 minute. Pour ½ cup of the pie filling into pie shell.

Slice 1 banana; arrange slices on filling in shell. Top with ¾ cup of the pie filling.

Blend whipped topping into remaining pie filling. Spread over filling in pie shell. Chill about 3 hours. Slice remaining banana; brush with lemon juice. Arrange banana slices on pie. Garnish with additional whipped topping, if desired.

— ■ —

LAYERED COOKIE PUDDING

Makes about 3 cups or 5 to 6 servings

4 cookies, coarsely crumbled
1 cup thawed COOL WHIP® Non-Dairy Whipped Topping
2 cups cold milk
1 package (4-serving size) JELL-O® Instant Pudding and
Pie Filling, any flavor

Gently fold cookies into whipped topping. Pour cold milk into bowl. Add pudding mix. With electric mixer at low speed, beat until well blended, 1 to 2 minutes. Pour half of the pudding into individual dessert glasses. Spoon 3 to 4 tablespoons of the whipped topping mixture over pudding in glasses. Spoon remaining pudding over whipped topping mixture. Garnish with additional whipped topping and halved cookies or whole strawberries, if desired.

PUDDING CHEESE PIE

Makes one 9-inch pie

1 package (8 ounces) cream cheese, softened
2 cups cold milk
1 package (4-serving size) JELL-O® Lemon, Coconut
    Cream, Vanilla or Pineapple Cream Flavor Instant
    Pudding and Pie Filling
1 prepared 9-inch graham cracker crumb crust or baked
    pie shell, cooled

With electric mixer at low speed, beat cream cheese until very soft. Gradually add ½ cup of the milk, beating until smooth. Add remaining milk and the pie filling mix, beating at low speed until blended, 1 minute. Pour immediately into pie crust. Chill until firm, about 2 hours. Sprinkle with nutmeg, if desired.

Sour Cream Cheese Pie: Prepare Pudding Cheese Pie as directed, using lemon flavor pudding and pie filling and substituting 1 cup sour cream for 1 cup of the milk.

Deluxe Lemon Pudding Cheese Pie: Prepare Pudding Cheese Pie as directed, using lemon flavor pudding and pie filling, increasing cream cheese to 11 to 12 ounces and adding 2 tablespoons sugar and ½ teaspoon vanilla with pie filling mix before beating.

Strawberry Almond Cheese Pie: Combine 1 cup sliced fresh strawberries, ¼ cup chopped toasted almonds and 1 tablespoon sugar. Spread in bottom of pie crust. Prepare Pudding Cheese Pie as directed, using vanilla flavor pudding and pie filling. Pour over strawberry mixture in pie crust. Garnish with whipped topping and additional strawberries, if desired.

Strawberry Cheese Pie: Prepare Pudding Cheese Pie as directed, using vanilla flavor pudding and pie filling, reducing milk to 1½ cups and folding in 1 cup sliced fresh strawberries. If desired, add a few drops of red food coloring to pie filling mixture before pouring into pie crust. Garnish with additional sliced strawberries, if desired.

Spicy Pudding Cheese Pie: Prepare Pudding Cheese Pie as directed, adding ¼ teaspoon cinnamon and ¼ teaspoon nutmeg.

Jelly Cheese Pie: Prepare Pudding Cheese Pie as directed, spreading about ½ cup jelly or jam on bottom of pie crust before pouring in filling.

Banana Pudding Cheese Pie: Prepare Pudding Cheese Pie as directed, adding 1 sliced banana to pie filling mixture before pouring into pie crust.

QUICK BAVARIAN

Makes 4 cups or 8 servings

- ¾ cup boiling water
- 1 package (4-serving size) JELL-O® Brand Gelatin, any flavor
- ½ cup cold water
  Ice cubes
- 1 cup thawed COOL WHIP® Non-Dairy Whipped Topping

Pour boiling water into blender. Add gelatin. Cover and blend at low speed until gelatin is completely dissolved, about 30 seconds. Combine cold water and ice cubes to make 1¼ cups. Add to gelatin and stir until ice is partially melted. Then add whipped topping; blend at high speed for 30 seconds. Pour into serving bowl. Chill 30 minutes.

POUND CAKE

Makes two 9 × 5-inch loaves

- 1 package (2-layer size) yellow cake mix or pudding-included cake mix
- 1 package (4-serving size) JELL-O® Vanilla, Butterscotch, Butter Pecan or Lemon Flavor Pudding and Pie Filling
- 1 cup (½ pint) sour cream or plain yogurt
- ⅓ cup vegetable oil
- 4 eggs
- ⅛ to ¼ teaspoon mace (optional)

Combine all ingredients in large bowl. With electric mixer at low speed, blend just to moisten, scraping sides of bowl often. Then beat at medium speed for 4 minutes. Pour batter into 2 greased and floured 9 × 5-inch loaf pans. Bake in preheated 350° oven for 40 to 45 minutes or until cake tester inserted in center of cakes comes out clean and cakes begin to pull away from sides of pans. Cool in pans on wire rack 15 minutes. Remove from pans and finish cooling on wire racks. Sprinkle with confectioners sugar, if desired.

Pound Cake ▶

Banana Split Pie (left), Pistachio Chocolate Crunch Pie (right)

PISTACHIO CHOCOLATE CRUNCH PIE

Makes one 9-inch pie

½ cup blanched almonds

2 cups (1 pint) sour cream

2 cups cold milk

1 package (4-serving size) JELL-O® Pistachio Flavor
   Instant Pudding and Pie Filling

1 baked 9-inch pie shell, cooled

1 cup thawed COOL WHIP® Non-Dairy Whipped Topping

1 cup graham cracker or vanilla or chocolate wafer
   crumbs

1 package (4-serving size) JELL-O® Chocolate Flavor
   Instant Pudding and Pie Filling

CONTINUED

Toast almonds in shallow pan in preheated 350° oven for 3 to 5 minutes, stirring once. Chop nuts; set aside. Place 1 cup of the sour cream and 1 cup of the milk in small bowl. Add pistachio flavor pie filling mix. With electric mixer at low speed, beat for 1 minute. Pour into pie shell. Spread whipped topping over filling; then sprinkle with nuts and crumbs.

Place remaining sour cream and remaining milk in another small bowl. Add chocolate flavor pie filling mix. With electric mixer at low speed, beat for 1 minute. Spoon over crumb layer. Chill about 4 hours. Garnish with additional whipped topping and multi-colored sprinkles, if desired.

BANANA SPLIT PIE

Makes one 9-inch pie

- 2 cups cold milk
- 1 package (4-serving size) JELL-O® Chocolate Flavor Instant Pudding and Pie Filling
- 1¾ cups thawed COOL WHIP® Non-Dairy Whipped Topping
- 1 baked 9-inch pie shell, cooled
- 1 medium banana, sliced
- 1 package (4-serving size) JELL-O® Vanilla Flavor Instant Pudding and Pie Filling
- 2 squares BAKER'S® Semi-Sweet Chocolate, melted

Pour 1 cup of the cold milk into bowl. Add chocolate flavor pie filling mix. With electric mixer at low speed, beat until blended, about 1 minute. Fold in 1 cup of the whipped topping. Pour into pie shell; top with banana slices.

Pour remaining cold milk into another bowl. Add vanilla flavor pie filling mix. With electric mixer at low speed, beat until blended, about 1 minute. Fold in remaining whipped topping. Pour over bananas in pie shell. Freeze or chill about 4 hours. Just before serving, drizzle with melted chocolate. Garnish with additional whipped topping and stemmed maraschino cherries, if desired.

— ◼ —

BURIED COOKIE DESSERT

Makes 8 to 10 servings

- 1 package (4-serving size) JELL-O® Brand Gelatin, any flavor
- ⅔ cup boiling water
- ½ cup cold water
- Ice cubes
- 3½ cups (8 ounces) COOL WHIP® Non-Dairy Whipped Topping, thawed
- 8 to 10 chocolate sandwich cookies

Completely dissolve gelatin in boiling water. Combine cold water and ice cubes to make 1¼ cups. Add to gelatin and stir until slightly thickened. Remove any unmelted ice. Using wire whisk, blend whipped topping into gelatin, then whip until smooth. Chill until mixture mounds, about 15 minutes. Crumble half of a cookie into each dessert glass. Spoon gelatin mixture over cookies in glasses, filling each glass only half full. Top with another crumbled cookie half. Spoon remaining gelatin mixture over cookies in glasses. Chill about 2 hours. Garnish with additional whipped topping and cookies, if desired.

THUMBPRINT COOKIES

Makes 3 dozen

1 package (4-serving size) JELL-O® Instant Pudding and
    Pie Filling, any flavor
1 package (10 ounces) pie crust mix
2 tablespoons butter or margarine, melted
4 to 5 tablespoons cold water
1 package (4 ounces) BAKER'S® GERMAN'S® Sweet
    Chocolate, broken into squares
    Whole or chopped toasted nuts

Combine pudding mix and pie crust mix in medium bowl; add butter and 4 tablespoons of the water. Mix with fork until soft dough forms. (If dough is too dry, add 1 tablespoon water.) Shape dough into 1-inch balls. Place 1 inch apart on ungreased baking sheets; press thumb deeply into center of each.

Cut each square of chocolate in half. Press 1 half into center of each cookie. Bake in preheated 350° oven for about 15 minutes or until lightly browned. Immediately press nuts lightly into chocolate centers. Remove from baking sheets and cool on wire racks.

Coconut Thumbprints: Prepare Thumbprint Cookies as directed, omitting chocolate and nuts. Mix 1⅓ cups (about) BAKER'S® ANGEL FLAKE® Coconut with ½ cup sweetened condensed milk; spoon into centers of cookies before baking.

Jam Thumbprints: Prepare Thumbprint Cookies as directed, omitting chocolate and nuts. Spoon ½ teaspoon jam into center of each cookie after baking.

Cream Cheese and Jelly Thumbprints: Prepare Thumbprint Cookies as directed, omitting chocolate and nuts. Using 1 package (3 ounces) cream cheese, softened, spoon ½ teaspoon cream cheese into center of each cookie before baking and top each with ½ teaspoon jelly after baking.

PUDDING ICE CREAM

Makes 6 cups or 12 servings

2 cups cold light cream or half and half
1 package (4-serving size) JELL-O® Vanilla or Chocolate
   Flavor Instant Pudding and Pie Filling
3½ cups (8 ounces) COOL WHIP® Non-Dairy Whipped
   Topping, thawed

Pour cold cream into bowl. Add pudding mix. With electric mixer at low speed, beat until well blended, 1 to 2 minutes. Let stand 5 minutes. Fold in whipped topping. Pour into 2-quart covered plastic container. Freeze until firm, about 6 hours.

Toffee Crunch Pudding Ice Cream: Prepare Pudding Ice Cream as directed, using vanilla flavor pudding mix and folding in ⅔ cup crushed chocolate-covered toffee bar with the whipped topping.

Rum Raisin Pudding Ice Cream: Prepare Pudding Ice Cream as directed, using vanilla flavor pudding mix. Soak ½ cup chopped raisins in 2 tablespoons light rum; fold in with the whipped topping.

Rocky Road Pudding Ice Cream: Prepare Pudding Ice Cream as directed, using chocolate flavor pudding mix and folding in 1 cup miniature marshmallows and ½ cup chopped walnuts with the whipped topping.

Cinnamon Walnut Pudding Ice Cream: Prepare Pudding Ice Cream as directed, using vanilla flavor pudding mix and adding 2 tablespoons light brown sugar and ½ teaspoon cinnamon to the pudding mix. Add ½ cup finely chopped walnuts with the whipped topping.

Fruit Pudding Ice Cream: Prepare Pudding Ice Cream as directed, folding in 1 cup pureed fruit (strawberries, peaches or raspberries) with the whipped topping.

Chocolate Chip Pudding Ice Cream: Prepare Pudding Ice Cream as directed, using chocolate flavor pudding mix and folding in ¾ cup BAKER'S® Real Semi-Sweet Chocolate Chips with the whipped topping.

BOSTON CREAM TORTE

Makes 1 cake

1 package (4-serving size) JELL-O® Banana Cream or
   Vanilla Flavor Pudding and Pie Filling

1¾ cups milk

2 baked 8-inch yellow cake layers, cooled

1 square BAKER'S® Unsweetened Chocolate

1 tablespoon butter or margarine

¾ cup confectioners sugar

1½ tablespoons hot milk

Dash salt

Combine pudding mix and milk in medium saucepan; blend well. Cook and stir over medium heat until mixture comes to a full boil. Cover with plastic wrap; chill. Split cake layers horizontally to make 4 thin layers. Beat pudding until creamy. Spread about ⅔ cup on each layer and stack.

Melt chocolate and butter in small saucepan over very low heat, stirring constantly. Combine sugar, hot milk and salt in bowl; add chocolate. Beat until smooth. Spread over top of cake. Chill. Store cake in refrigerator.

LEMON SUNDAE PIE

Makes one 9-inch pie

2 cups cold milk

2 packages (4-serving size) JELL-O® Lemon Flavor Instant
Pudding and Pie Filling

3½ cups (8 ounces) COOL WHIP® Non-Dairy Whipped
Topping, thawed

1 prepared 9-inch graham cracker crumb crust, cooled

1 can (21 ounces) cherry pie filling

Pour cold milk into bowl. Add pie filling mixes. With electric mixer at low
speed, beat until blended, about 1 minute. Fold in whipped topping. Pour
into shallow pan; freeze until firm, about 4 hours. Let stand at room
temperature 10 to 15 minutes; then scoop lemon pie filling into pie crust.
Freeze about 1 hour. Spoon cherry pie filling over frozen filling in pie crust.
Let stand at room temperature 10 to 15 minutes before serving.

— ■ —

MICROWAVE FAST FUDGE

Makes 21 pieces

3 tablespoons butter or margarine

1 package (4-serving size) JELL-O® Vanilla Flavor Pudding
   and Pie Filling

⅓ cup milk

½ teaspoon vanilla

¼ teaspoon salt

2 cups confectioners sugar, sifted

⅓ cup chopped walnuts

⅓ cup BAKER'S® Real Semi-Sweet Chocolate Chips

Microwave:* Heat butter in 1½-quart microwave-safe bowl at HIGH 35 seconds or until melted. Stir in pudding mix and milk. Cook 2 minutes longer or until mixture begins to boil, stirring every 30 seconds. Stir in vanilla and salt. With electric mixer at low speed, beat in sugar, 1 cup at a time, until smooth. (Mixture will be stiff.) Fold in nuts and chocolate. Press fudge evenly into 8×4-inch loaf pan that has been lined with waxed paper. Cover and chill until firm. Cut into squares.

Microwave Chocolate Mallow Fudge: Prepare Microwave Fast Fudge as directed, substituting chocolate flavor pudding and pie filling and ⅓ cup miniature marshmallows for the vanilla flavor pudding and the walnuts.

Microwave S'Mores Fudge: Prepare Microwave Fast Fudge as directed, substituting ⅓ cup each crushed graham crackers, miniature marshmallows and chunks of BAKER'S® Semi-Sweet Chocolate for the walnuts and chocolate chips.

Microwave Coconut Macaroon Fudge: Prepare Microwave Fast Fudge as directed, substituting almond extract and ⅓ cup BAKER'S® ANGEL FLAKE® Coconut for the vanilla and walnuts. Omit chocolate chips.

*Ovens vary. Cooking time is approximate.

— ■ —

The youngsters will really enjoy these fun and colorful snacks and desserts. From casual goodies to special treats, the kid-pleasing recipes are sure to be a hit! Many are even easy enough for small hands to whip up!

Gelatin Jiggles

GELATIN JIGGLES

Makes about 1½ dozen cutouts

4 packages (4-serving size) or 2 packages (8-serving size)
JELL-O® Brand Gelatin, any flavor
2½ cups boiling water or fruit juice

Completely dissolve gelatin in boiling water. Pour into 9-inch square pan. Chill until firm, about 4 hours. Cut with small cookie cutters that have been dipped in warm water, or cut into 1-inch squares. Carefully transfer cutouts to serving plates, using broad spatula that has been dipped in warm water. Flake remaining gelatin with fork.

Note: To cut letters or shapes, place paper or cardboard pattern on firm gelatin; cut with sharp knife that has been dipped in warm water.

FROZEN CHOCOLATE GRAHAM CUPS

Makes about 4 cups or 8 servings

1½ cups cold milk
1 package (4-serving size) JELL-O® Chocolate Flavor
   Instant Pudding and Pie Filling
1 cup thawed COOL WHIP® Non-Dairy Whipped Topping
7 whole graham crackers, broken in pieces
½ cup miniature marshmallows
¼ cup chopped salted peanuts

Pour cold milk into bowl. Add pudding mix. With electric mixer at low speed, beat until well blended, 1 to 2 minutes. Let stand 5 minutes. Fold in whipped topping, crackers, marshmallows and peanuts. Spoon into muffin pan lined with paper baking cups. Freeze until firm, about 3 hours. Garnish with additional whipped topping, if desired.

Frozen Vanilla Graham Cups: Prepare Frozen Chocolate Graham Cups as directed, substituting vanilla flavor instant pudding and pie filling for the chocolate flavor pudding and ¼ cup chopped nuts or slivered almonds and ¼ cup diced maraschino cherries for the marshmallows and peanuts. Makes 3 cups or 6 servings.

MARSHMALLOW PARFAIT

Makes about 2 cups or 4 servings

1 package (4-serving size) JELL-O® Brand Gelatin, any
   flavor
1 cup boiling water
1 cup cold water
   Miniature marshmallows

Dissolve gelatin in boiling water. Add cold water. Measure ⅔ cup of the gelatin; chill until slightly thickened. With electric mixer at medium speed, beat measured gelatin until fluffy, thick and about doubled in volume. Chill until set.

Chill remaining gelatin until set; spoon half of remaining gelatin into parfait glasses. Add a layer of marshmallows. Spoon whipped gelatin over marshmallows in glasses; top with remaining clear gelatin. Chill. Garnish with additional marshmallows, if desired.

PUDDING CONES

Makes about 2 cups or 4 servings

1 cup cold milk
1 package (4-serving size) JELL-O® Chocolate or Vanilla
   Flavor Instant Pudding and Pie Filling
1 cup thawed COOL WHIP® Non-Dairy Whipped Topping
¼ cup chopped nuts or peanuts (optional)
4 ice cream wafer cups

Pour cold milk into bowl. Add pudding mix. With electric mixer at low speed, beat until well blended, 1 to 2 minutes. Blend in whipped topping and nuts. Chill. Just before serving, spoon pudding mixture into wafer cups. Garnish with additional whipped topping and nuts or assorted candies or maraschino cherries, if desired.

Note: For a party, make individual clown faces. Scoop pudding onto dessert plates. Substitute sugar cones for wafer cups and place on top of pudding for a clown hat. Use coconut for hair and fruit for eyes, nose and mouth.

GELATIN BANANA SPLITS

Makes 3 or 4 servings

1 package (4-serving size) JELL-O® Brand Gelatin, any
   flavor
1 cup boiling water
1 cup cold water
3 or 4 medium bananas
   Lemon juice
½ cup thawed COOL WHIP® Non-Dairy Whipped Topping
3 or 4 maraschino cherries
   Chopped nuts

Dissolve gelatin in boiling water. Add cold water and pour into deep narrow
bowl. Chill until firm. Just before serving, cut bananas in half lengthwise;
brush with lemon juice and arrange in banana-split dishes. Scoop gelatin
onto bananas. Garnish with whipped topping, cherries and nuts.

SHAKER ADD-IN PUDDING

Makes 2⅓ cups or 4 servings

2 cups cold milk
1 package (4-serving size) JELL-O® Instant Pudding and
    Pie Filling, any flavor
    Add-Ins*

Pour cold milk into 1-quart container with tight-fitting lid. Add pudding mix. Cover tightly. Holding container on top and bottom, shake hard for 45 seconds. Let stand 1 to 2 minutes. Stir in Add-Ins. Pour into individual dessert glasses. Garnish with additional Add-Ins, if desired.

*Suggested Add-Ins
Use ½ cup chocolate or butterscotch chips.

Use ½ cup raisins, coarsely chopped nuts or miniature marshmallows.

Use ½ cup crushed cookies, BAKER'S® ANGEL FLAKE® Coconut or small candies.

QUICK PUDDING COOKIES

Makes about 2 dozen

1 package (4-serving size) JELL-O® Instant Pudding and
 Pie Filling, any flavor
1 cup all-purpose biscuit mix
¼ cup vegetable oil
1 egg, slightly beaten
3 tablespoons water

Combine pudding mix and biscuit mix in medium bowl. Stir in oil, egg and water, blending well. Drop from teaspoon 2 inches apart onto ungreased baking sheets. Bake in preheated 375° oven for about 12 minutes, or until lightly browned. Remove from baking sheets and cool on wire racks. Store in tightly covered container.

Quick Pudding Chip Cookies: Prepare Quick Pudding Cookies as directed, stirring in ½ cup BAKER'S® Semi-Sweet Chocolate Flavored Chips just before baking. Makes 2½ dozen cookies.

Note: Cookie dough may be pressed through cookie press, or rolled into 1-inch balls and flattened on baking sheets with fork or glass dipped in flour; reduce water to 2 tablespoons.

ICE CREAM AND ORANGE DESSERT

Makes about 3 cups or 6 servings

¾ cup boiling water
1 package (4-serving size) JELL-O® Brand Orange, Peach or
 Lemon Flavor Gelatin
1 cup (½ pint) vanilla ice cream
½ cup crushed ice
1 medium orange, peeled and cut into bite-size pieces

Pour boiling water into blender. Add gelatin. Cover and blend at low speed until gelatin is completely dissolved, about 30 seconds. Add ice cream and crushed ice. Blend at high speed until ice is melted, about 30 seconds. Pour into bowl. Stir in orange. Chill until firm, about 1 hour. When ready to serve, spoon into flat-bottom ice cream cups or dessert dishes.

GELATIN FRUIT BOUQUET

Makes about 4 cups or 8 servings

1 jar (16 or 17 ounces) fruits for salad
  Chives or scallions
2 packages (4-serving size) or 1 package (8-serving size)
  JELL-O® Brand Orange Flavor Gelatin
1 cup cold water
  Ice cubes

Drain fruit, reserving syrup. Add water to syrup to make 1½ cups. Arrange fruit on bottom of 9-inch cake pan, using pear pieces to resemble woven basket. Cut peaches into pieces to make daffodils and use cherries for center of flowers. Use either chives or scallions for stems.

Place measured liquid in small saucepan. Bring to a boil over high heat. Completely dissolve gelatin in boiling liquid. Combine cold water and ice cubes to make 2½ cups. Add to gelatin, stirring until slightly thickened. Remove any unmelted ice. Measure 1 cup of the gelatin; pour into another 9-inch cake pan. Quickly transfer arrangement of fruits onto gelatin. Carefully spoon remaining gelatin over fruit. Chill overnight. Unmold. Serve with any remaining fruit.

Note: Fruits may be arranged to resemble a face or decorative pattern.

CHOCOLATE PEANUT BUTTER DESSERT

Makes about 3 cups or 6 servings

2 cups plus 3 tablespoons cold milk
3 tablespoons creamy peanut butter
1 cup thawed COOL WHIP® Non-Dairy Whipped Topping
1 package (4-serving size) JELL-O® Chocolate Flavor
  Instant Pudding and Pie Filling

Blend 3 tablespoons of the milk with peanut butter, stirring until smooth. Fold in whipped topping. Pour remaining cold milk into another bowl. Add pudding mix. With electric mixer at low speed, beat until well blended, 1 to 2 minutes. Alternately spoon whipped topping mixture and pudding into individual parfait glasses. Chill.

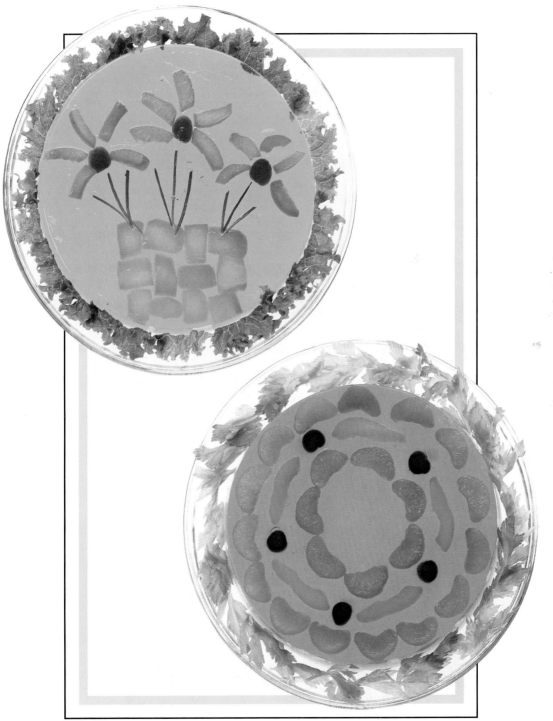

Gelatin Fruit Bouquet

BANANA MALLOW DESSERT

Makes about 3 cups or 6 servings

1 large banana, sliced*
1 cup miniature marshmallows
1 package (4-serving size) JELL-O® Brand Gelatin, any red flavor
¾ cup boiling water
½ cup cold water
　Ice cubes

Arrange banana slices and marshmallows in dessert glasses or serving bowl; set aside. Completely dissolve gelatin in boiling water. Combine cold water and ice cubes to make 1¼ cups. Add to gelatin, stirring until slightly thickened. Remove any unmelted ice. Pour over banana and marshmallows. Chill until set, about 30 minutes.

*Substitution: Use 1 cup fresh or canned peach slices or 1 cup sliced strawberries.

ROCKY ROAD PUDDING

Makes 3 cups or 6 servings

2 cups cold milk
1 package (4-serving size) JELL-O® Chocolate Flavor Instant Pudding and Pie Filling
½ cup miniature marshmallows
⅓ cup unsalted peanuts, coarsely chopped
⅓ cup BAKER'S® Real Semi-Sweet Chocolate Chips

Pour cold milk into bowl. Add pudding mix. With electric mixer at low speed, beat until well blended, 1 to 2 minutes. Let stand 5 minutes. Fold in marshmallows, peanuts and chocolate chips. Spoon into individual dessert dishes. Chill about 2 hours. Garnish with whipped topping and additional chopped peanuts, if desired.

— ■ —

FRUIT-FLAVOR POPCORN

Makes 2 quarts

8 cups popped popcorn
¼ cup butter or margarine, melted
1 package (4-serving size) JELL-O® Brand Gelatin, any
   flavor

Place popcorn in large bowl. Add melted butter; toss to coat. Sprinkle with gelatin; toss until evenly coated.

PUDDING PIZZA

Makes 10 to 12 servings

1 package (17 ounces) refrigerated sugar cookie dough
1¼ cups cold milk
1 package (4-serving size) JELL-O® Vanilla or French
   Vanilla Flavor Instant Pudding and Pie Filling
1 cup thawed COOL WHIP® Non-Dairy Whipped Topping
2 cups (about) fresh fruit (sliced strawberries, halved
   seedless grapes, blueberries)*
2 tablespoons (about) melted currant jelly*

Cut cookie dough into ¼-inch slices. Arrange slices on ungreased 12-inch pizza pan so that sides are touching. Press dough together so that there are no cracks in dough. Bake in preheated 350° oven for 15 minutes or until golden brown. Cool on wire rack, then chill.

Pour cold milk into bowl. Add pudding mix. With electric mixer at low speed, beat until well blended, 1 to 2 minutes. Let stand 5 minutes. Fold in whipped topping. Shortly before serving, evenly spread pudding mixture over crust. Arrange fruits on top and brush lightly with jelly. Chill 5 to 10 minutes.

*Substitution: Use ½ cup BAKER'S® Semi-Sweet Chocolate Flavored Chips, ½ cup miniature marshmallows and ¼ cup chopped pecans, omitting jelly.

— —

CREAMY BANANA SPLITS

Makes 4 servings

2 cups cold milk

1 package (4-serving size) JELL-O® Milk Chocolate, Coconut Cream, Pineapple Cream or Vanilla Flavor Instant Pudding and Pie Filling

4 medium bananas
  Lemon juice

½ cup thawed COOL WHIP® Non-Dairy Whipped Topping

4 maraschino cherries
  Chocolate syrup
  Toasted flaked coconut
  Chopped nuts

Pour cold milk into bowl. Add pudding mix. With electric mixer at low speed, beat until well blended, 1 to 2 minutes. Chill. Just before serving, cut bananas in half lengthwise; brush with lemon juice and arrange in banana-split dishes. Stir pudding until creamy and spoon over bananas in mounds. Garnish with whipped topping, cherries, syrup, coconut and nuts.

BOSTON CREAM PARFAIT

Makes about 3 cups or 6 servings

2 cups cold milk

1 package (4-serving size) JELL-O® Vanilla Flavor Instant
   Pudding and Pie Filling

2 tablespoons chocolate syrup

1 cup thawed COOL WHIP® Non-Dairy Whipped Topping

Pour cold milk into bowl. Add pudding mix. With electric mixer at low speed, beat until well blended, 1 to 2 minutes. Pour half of the pudding into 6 parfait glasses. Top with chocolate syrup, spooning syrup along edge of glasses. Then top with whipped topping and remaining pudding. Chill. Garnish with additional chocolate syrup and whipped topping, if desired.

Luscious Fruity Sundae

LUSCIOUS FRUITY SUNDAE

Makes 4 servings

- 1 package (4-serving size) JELL-O® Brand Gelatin, any flavor
- ¾ cup boiling water
- ½ cup cold water
  Ice cubes
- 2 cups (1 pint) ice cream, any flavor
- ½ cup fruit sundae sauce or drained fruit (optional)
- 1 cup thawed COOL WHIP® Non-Dairy Whipped Topping
- ¼ cup chopped nuts (optional)
- 4 stemmed maraschino cherries

Completely dissolve gelatin in boiling water. Combine cold water and ice cubes to make 1¼ cups. Add to gelatin, stirring until slightly thickened. Remove any unmelted ice. Alternately spoon ice cream and gelatin into tall sundae glasses, ending with gelatin and filling to within ½ inch of the top of the glass. Top with sauce, whipped topping, nuts and a cherry.

FROZEN PUDDING SANDWICHES

Makes 12 sandwiches

- 1½ cups cold milk
- ½ cup peanut butter (optional)*
- 1 package (4-serving size) JELL-O® Instant Pudding and Pie Filling, any flavor
- 24 graham cracker squares*

Gradually add milk to peanut butter in bowl, blending until smooth. Add pudding mix. With electric mixer at low speed, beat until well blended, 1 to 2 minutes. Let stand 5 minutes. Spread filling about ½ inch thick on 12 of the graham cracker squares. Top with remaining squares, pressing lightly and smoothing around edges with spatula. Freeze until firm, about 3 hours. Sandwiches can be stored, wrapped, in freezer 3 to 4 days.

*When omitting peanut butter, reduce squares to 18; makes 9 sandwiches.

OFF THE SHELF

When you need a spur-of-the-moment
inspiration, create an out-of-the-ordinary delight
with everyday ingredients you have
on hand. These scrumptious stock-ups
will be the star of any meal!

Cup of Trifle

CUP OF TRIFLE

Makes about 3½ cups or 6 servings

1½ cups ½-inch pound cake cubes

  2 tablespoons orange juice

  3 tablespoons raspberry preserves

  1 tablespoon water

1½ cups cold milk

  1 package (4-serving size) JELL-O® French Vanilla or
     Vanilla Instant Pudding and Pie Filling*

1¾ cups thawed COOL WHIP® Non-Dairy Whipped Topping

  1 tablespoon sherry wine (optional)*

Arrange cake cubes in individual dessert glasses; sprinkle with orange juice. Combine raspberry preserves with water. Spoon over cake cubes.

Pour cold milk into bowl. Add pudding mix. With electric mixer at low speed, beat until well blended, 1 to 2 minutes. Blend in 1 cup of the whipped topping and the sherry. Spoon over preserves in glasses. Chill. Garnish with remaining whipped topping, stemmed maraschino cherries and toasted slivered almonds, if desired.

*Substitution: Use chocolate flavor instant pudding and pie filling and 2 tablespoons almond liqueur.

PUDDING COOKIE BARS

Makes about 6 dozen

  1 package (2-layer size) yellow cake mix or pudding-
     included cake mix

  1 package (4-serving size) JELL-O® Vanilla Flavor Instant
     Pudding and Pie Filling

  2 eggs

  ½ cup vegetable oil

  ¼ cup water

Combine all ingredients in large bowl; stir with spoon until well blended. Spread in well-greased 15×10-inch jelly-roll pan. Bake in preheated 350° oven for 25 to 30 minutes. Cool completely in pan on wire rack; then cut into bars.

APRICOT CHIFFON

Makes about 4 cups or 8 servings

1 can (8½ ounces) apricot halves in light syrup
¾ cup boiling water
1 package (4-serving size) JELL-O® Brand Apricot Flavor
    Gelatin
1 teaspoon grated lemon rind (optional)
1 tablespoon lemon juice
    Ice cubes
1¾ cups thawed COOL WHIP® Non-Dairy Whipped Topping

Drain apricots, reserving syrup. Combine syrup and water to make ½ cup; set aside. Dice apricots and divide among individual parfait glasses. Pour boiling water into blender. Add gelatin, lemon rind and lemon juice. Cover and blend at low speed until gelatin is completely dissolved, about 30 seconds. Combine measured liquid and ice cubes to make 1¼ cups. Add to gelatin and stir until ice is partially melted. Then add whipped topping; blend at high speed 30 seconds. Pour over fruit in glasses. Chill until set, about 30 minutes. Garnish with additional whipped topping and fruit, if desired.

Orange-Pineapple Chiffon: Prepare Apricot Chiffon as directed, substituting 1 can (8¼ ounces) crushed pineapple in juice and orange-pineapple flavor gelatin for the apricots and apricot flavor gelatin.

Peach Chiffon: Prepare Apricot Chiffon as directed, substituting 1 can (8¼ to 8¾ ounces) sliced peaches and peach flavor gelatin for the apricots and apricot flavor gelatin.

— ■ —

FROZEN PEANUT BUTTER PIE

Makes one 9-inch pie

3½ cups (8 ounces) COOL WHIP® Non-Dairy Whipped
    Topping, thawed
1 prepared 9-inch graham cracker crumb crust, cooled
⅓ cup strawberry jam
1 cup cold milk
½ cup chunky peanut butter
1 package (4-serving size) JELL-O® Vanilla Flavor Instant
    Pudding and Pie Filling

Spread 1 cup of the whipped topping in bottom of pie crust; freeze for about 10 minutes. Carefully spoon jam over whipped topping.

Gradually add milk to peanut butter in bowl, blending until smooth. Add pie filling mix. With electric mixer at low speed, beat until well blended, 1 to 2 minutes. Fold in remaining whipped topping. Spoon over jam in pie crust. Freeze until firm, about 4 hours. Garnish with additional whipped topping and chopped nuts, if desired.

FRUITED MARBLE DESSERT

Makes about 5 cups or 10 servings

2 packages (4-serving size) or 1 package (8-serving size)
   JELL-O® Brand Strawberry or Strawberry-Banana
   Flavor Gelatin*

1½ cups boiling water

1 cup cold canned pineapple juice*
   Ice cubes

1 cup (½ pint) vanilla ice cream*

1 cup sliced or diced strawberries*

Completely dissolve gelatin in boiling water. Combine juice and ice cubes
to make 2½ cups. Add to gelatin, stirring until slightly thickened. Remove
any unmelted ice. Measure 1 cup of the thickened gelatin and stir in ice

CONTINUED

— ■ —

cream. Let stand a few minutes to thicken even more. Stir fruit into remaining gelatin. Spoon about a third of the fruited gelatin into individual dessert glasses or serving bowl. Spoon half of the creamy mixture over fruited gelatin. Repeat layers, then spoon remaining fruited gelatin on top. Chill until set, about 1 hour. Garnish as desired.

*Additional Combinations
Use orange flavor gelatin with orange juice, 1 cup whipped topping and ½ cup each diced oranges and bananas.

Use raspberry flavor gelatin with apple juice, 1 package (3 ounces) softened cream cheese beaten with 1 tablespoon milk, ¾ cup diced apples, ¼ cup chopped celery and 2 tablespoons chopped nuts.

Use lime flavor gelatin with orange juice, 1 package (3 ounces) softened cream cheese beaten with 1 tablespoon milk and 1 large diced peeled fresh pear.

LAYERED ORANGE WHIP

Makes 4 cups or 6 servings

>   1 can (11 ounces) mandarin orange sections
>   1 package (4-serving size) JELL-O® Brand Orange Flavor
>   Gelatin
>   ½ cup cold water
>   Ice cubes

Drain orange sections, reserving syrup. Place orange sections in dessert glasses. Add water to syrup to make ¾ cup; bring to a boil over high heat. Pour boiling syrup mixture into blender. Add gelatin. Cover and blend at low speed until gelatin is completely dissolved, about 30 seconds. Combine cold water and ice cubes to make 1¼ cups. Add to gelatin and stir until ice is partially melted; then blend at high speed for 30 seconds. Pour over orange sections. Do not stir. Chill until firm, 20 to 30 minutes. Dessert layers as it chills.

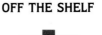

FRUIT AND JUICE PUDDING

Makes 3 cups or 6 servings

1 can (17 ounces) fruit cocktail
1 package (4-serving size) JELL-O® Vanilla Flavor Pudding
  and Pie Filling
1⅔ cups milk

Microwave:* Drain fruit cocktail, reserving ⅓ cup syrup; set aside. Combine pudding mix and milk in 1½-quart microwave-safe bowl; blend well. Add reserved syrup. Cook at HIGH 3 minutes. Stir well and cook 2 minutes longer; then stir again and cook 1 minute or until mixture comes to a boil. Cover surface of pudding with plastic wrap. Chill. Fold in fruit. Spoon into individual dessert dishes.

*Ovens vary. Cooking time is approximate.

FLUFFY PUDDING PIE

Makes one 9-inch pie

2 envelopes DREAM WHIP® Whipped Topping Mix
2¾ cups cold milk
2 packages (4-serving size) JELL-O® Instant Pudding and
  Pie Filling, any flavor*
1 baked 9-inch pie shell, cooled

Combine whipped topping mix and 1 cup of the milk in large bowl. With electric mixer at high speed, beat until topping peaks, about 2 minutes. Then beat 2 minutes longer until topping is light and fluffy. Add remaining milk and the pie filling mix. Blend at low speed until just combined; then beat at high speed for 2 minutes, scraping bowl occasionally. Spoon into pie shell. Chill about 4 hours. Garnish with fruit, if desired.

Note: For chocolate, chocolate fudge, pistachio and butter pecan flavors, add ½ teaspoon almond extract with the milk, if desired.

Fluffy Mocha Pie: Prepare Fluffy Pudding Pie as directed, using chocolate or chocolate fudge pudding and pie filling and adding 3 tablespoons MAXWELL HOUSE® or YUBAN® Instant Coffee dissolved in 3 tablespoons water with the pie filling mix.

—■—

GINGER PINEAPPLE MOLD

Makes 5 cups or 10 servings

1 can (20 ounces) pineapple slices in juice
2 packages (4-serving size) or 1 package (8-serving size)
    JELL-O® Brand Lime or Apricot Flavor Gelatin
1½ cups boiling water
1 cup ginger ale or cold water
¼ teaspoon ginger

Drain pineapple, reserving juice. Cut 4 pineapple slices in half; set aside. Cut remaining pineapple slices into chunks. Dissolve gelatin in boiling water. Add reserved juice, ginger ale and ginger. Chill until slightly thickened. Measure 1 cup of the gelatin. Arrange some of the pineapple chunks in 6-cup ring mold; top with measured gelatin. Chill until set but not firm, about 10 minutes. Fold remaining pineapple chunks into remaining gelatin; spoon over gelatin in mold. Chill until firm, about 4 hours. Unmold. Garnish with halved pineapple slices, halved cherry tomatoes and crisp greens, if desired.

—■—

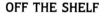

MANDARIN PARFAITS

Makes 6 servings

1 cup cold milk
1 cup (½ pint) sour cream
¼ teaspoon almond extract
1 package (4-serving size) JELL-O® Vanilla or French
    Vanilla Flavor Instant Pudding and Pie Filling
1 can (11 ounces) mandarin orange sections, drained

Combine milk, sour cream and almond extract in bowl. Add pudding mix. With electric mixer at low speed, beat until well blended, 1 to 2 minutes. Layer pudding and orange sections in individual parfait glasses. Chill about 1 hour. Garnish with whipped topping, if desired.

CREAMY FRUIT PUDDING

Makes about 4 cups or 8 servings

1 can (16 to 17 ounces) sliced peaches, fruit cocktail,
    apricot halves or peach halves
1 cup cold milk
1 package (4-serving size) JELL-O® Vanilla or Lemon
    Flavor Instant Pudding and Pie Filling
1 envelope DREAM WHIP® Whipped Topping Mix

Drain peaches, reserving syrup. Add cold water to syrup to make 1 cup; set aside. Dice peaches, reserving 2 tablespoons for garnish, if desired.

Pour cold milk into bowl. Add pudding mix and whipped topping mix. With electric mixer at low speed, beat until thoroughly blended. Add measured liquid and beat at medium speed for 3 minutes. Fold peaches into pudding mixture; spoon into individual dessert dishes. Garnish with reserved diced peaches. Chill about 1 hour.

Mandarin Parfaits

SOUR CREAM PUDDING

Makes about 2 cups or 4 servings

1 package (4-serving size) JELL-O® Pudding and Pie Filling,
   any flavor except lemon
3 tablespoons sugar
1 cup water
1 cup (½ pint) sour cream

Range Top: Combine pudding mix, sugar and water in medium saucepan; blend well. Cook and stir over medium heat until mixture comes to a full boil. Cool 5 minutes, stirring twice. Stir in sour cream, blending well. Pour into bowl or dessert glasses. Chill. Garnish with whipped topping, and sprinkle with nutmeg or chocolate curls, if desired.

Microwave:* Combine pudding mix, sugar and water in 1½-quart microwave-safe bowl; blend well. Cook at HIGH 3 minutes. Stir well and cook 2 minutes longer; then stir again and cook 1 minute or until mixture comes to a boil. Cool 5 minutes, stirring twice. Stir in sour cream, blending well. Pour into bowl or dessert glasses. Chill. Garnish with whipped topping, and sprinkle with nutmeg or chocolate curls, if desired.

*Ovens vary. Cooking time is approximate.

FOAMY PEACH DESSERT

Makes 3½ cups or 6 or 7 servings

1 can (8¾ ounces) sliced peaches in light syrup
1 package (4-serving size) JELL-O® Brand Gelatin, any
   flavor
1½ cups ice cubes

Drain peaches, reserving syrup. Add water to syrup to make ¾ cup; pour into small saucepan. Bring to a boil over high heat. Pour boiling liquid into blender. Add gelatin. Cover and blend at high speed until gelatin is completely dissolved, about 1 minute. Add ice cubes and stir until ice is partially melted. Add peaches. Blend at high speed for 2 minutes or until ice is melted and mixture is smooth. Pour into serving bowl or individual dessert dishes. Chill until set, about 2 hours.

— ■ —

RIPPLE DESSERT

Makes about 2½ cups or 5 servings

2 cups cold milk
1 package (4-serving size) JELL-O® Vanilla Flavor Instant
  Pudding and Pie Filling
1 cup thawed COOL WHIP® Non-Dairy Whipped Topping
3 tablespoons chocolate syrup*

Pour cold milk into bowl. Add pudding mix. With electric mixer at low speed, beat until well blended, 1 to 2 minutes. Fold in whipped topping. Layer pudding mixture and syrup in individual parfait glasses. Chill. Garnish with additional whipped topping and syrup, if desired.

*Substitution: Use ¼ cup raspberry or strawberry preserves thinned with ½ teaspoon water.

CHOCOLATE MOUSSE

Makes about 3 cups or 6 servings

1 package (4-serving size) JELL-O® Chocolate Flavor
  Pudding and Pie Filling
1 cup milk
2 or 3 squares BAKER'S® Semi-Sweet Chocolate
1¾ cups thawed COOL WHIP® Non-Dairy Whipped Topping

Combine pudding mix and milk in medium saucepan; blend well. Add chocolate. Cook and stir over medium heat until mixture comes to a full boil. Pour into bowl; cover surface of pudding with plastic wrap. Cool to room temperature. With electric mixer at low speed, beat chocolate mixture and whipped topping until well blended. Spoon into individual dessert dishes. Chill.

— ■ —

PUDDING COOKIE SURPRISE

Makes 4 servings

1 package (4-serving size) JELL-O® Pudding and Pie Filling,
   any flavor
2 cups milk
6 gingersnaps, crumbled
⅓ cup chopped nuts
2 tablespoons butter or margarine, melted

Range Top: Combine pudding mix and milk in medium saucepan; blend well. Cook and stir over medium heat until mixture comes to a full boil. Pour into bowl; cover surface of pudding with plastic wrap. Chill.

Combine crumbs, nuts and butter; mix well. Place about 2 tablespoons of the crumb mixture into each of 4 dessert dishes. Stir pudding and spoon into dishes. Sprinkle with remaining crumb mixture.

Microwave:* Combine pudding mix and milk in 1½-quart microwave-safe bowl; blend well. Cook at HIGH 3 minutes. Stir well and cook 2 minutes longer; then stir again and cook 1 minute or until mixture comes to a boil. Stir; cover surface of pudding with plastic wrap. Chill.

Combine crumbs, nuts and butter; mix well. Place about 2 tablespoons of the crumb mixture into each of 4 dessert dishes. Stir pudding and spoon into dishes. Sprinkle with remaining crumb mixture.

*Ovens vary. Cooking time is approximate.

FRUITED CHIFFON SQUARES

Makes about 4½ cups or 9 servings

2 packages (4-serving size) or 1 package (8-serving size)
   JELL-O® Brand Gelatin, any flavor
1½ cups boiling water
1 cup cold water
   Ice cubes
1¾ cups thawed COOL WHIP® Non-Dairy Whipped Topping
1 can (8 to 8½ ounces) fruit, drained, or 1 cup sliced or
   diced fresh fruit*

CONTINUED

Completely dissolve gelatin in boiling water. Combine cold water and ice cubes to make 2½ cups. Add to gelatin, stirring until slightly thickened. Remove any unmelted ice. Measure 1 cup of the gelatin; fold into whipped topping. Pour into 8-inch square pan. Chill about 10 minutes. Add fruit to remaining gelatin; gently spoon over creamy layer in pan. Chill until firm, about 3 hours. Cut into squares. Garnish as desired.

*Do not use fresh pineapple, kiwifruit, mango, papaya or figs.

LIGHT AND FRUITY PIE

Makes one 9-inch pie

1 package (4-serving size) JELL-O® Brand Gelatin, any flavor

⅔ cup boiling water

½ cup cold water
Ice cubes

3½ cups (8 ounces) COOL WHIP® Non-Dairy Whipped Topping, thawed

1 cup diced peeled fresh peaches, apricots or pears*

1 prepared 9-inch graham cracker crumb crust, cooled

Completely dissolve gelatin in boiling water. Combine cold water and ice cubes to make 1¼ cups. Add to gelatin, stirring until slightly thickened.

CONTINUED

Remove any unmelted ice. Using wire whisk, blend in whipped topping. Fold in fruit. Chill until mixture mounds. Spoon into pie crust. Chill about 2 hours. Garnish with additional fruit, if desired.

*Substitutions:
Use 1 cup fresh raspberries or blueberries or halved pitted dark sweet cherries.

Use 1 cup diced orange sections, banana or strawberries.

Use ½ cup each sliced banana, diced peeled pear and halved seedless grapes.

Use ½ cup each toasted slivered almonds and halved seedless grapes.

Use 1 can (8¾ ounces) apricots or sliced peaches, drained and diced.

Use 1 can (8¼ ounces) crushed pineapple, drained.

Use 1 can (8¾ ounces) fruit cocktail, drained.

FLUFFY RASPBERRY PARFAIT

Makes about 2½ cups or 5 servings

1½ **cups cold milk**
1 **envelope DREAM WHIP® Whipped Topping Mix**
¼ **teaspoon almond extract**
1 **package (4-serving size) JELL-O® Vanilla Flavor Instant Pudding and Pie Filling**
⅓ **cup raspberry jam**

Combine ½ cup of the cold milk and the whipped topping mix in bowl. With electric mixer at low speed, beat until blended. Beat at high speed for about 4 minutes or until topping thickens and forms peaks, scraping bowl often. Add remaining milk, the extract and pudding mix. Blend; then beat at high speed for 2 minutes. Spoon half of the pudding mixture into individual dessert dishes. Add about 1 tablespoon jam to each glass. Top with remaining pudding mixture. Chill 30 minutes. Garnish with additional jam, if desired.

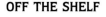

LEMON CHIFFON

Makes about 4 cups or 8 servings

¾ cup boiling water
1 package (4-serving size) JELL-O® Brand Lemon Flavor
    Gelatin
1 teaspoon grated lemon rind (optional)
1 tablespoon lemon juice
½ cup cold water
    Ice cubes
1¾ cups thawed COOL WHIP® Non-Dairy Whipped Topping

Pour boiling water into blender. Add gelatin, lemon rind and lemon juice. Cover and blend at low speed until gelatin is completely dissolved, about 30 seconds. Combine cold water and ice cubes to make 1¼ cups. Add to gelatin and stir until ice is partially melted. Then add whipped topping; blend at high speed for 30 seconds. Pour into serving bowl or dessert dishes. Chill until set, about 1 hour. Garnish with additional whipped topping and thin lemon slices, if desired.

Lime Chiffon: Prepare Lemon Chiffon as directed, substituting lime flavor gelatin, lime rind and lime juice for the lemon flavor gelatin, rind and juice.

Orange Chiffon: Grate 1 teaspoon rind from 1 medium orange; set aside. Peel, section and dice orange; divide among 8 parfait glasses. Prepare Lemon Chiffon as directed, substituting orange flavor gelatin and orange rind for the lemon flavor gelatin and rind. Omit the lemon juice.

CREAMY PUDDING FREEZE

Makes about 3 cups or 6 servings

1 cup cold milk
1 package (4-serving size) JELL-O® Instant Pudding and
    Pie Filling, any flavor
1¾ cups thawed COOL WHIP® Non-Dairy Whipped Topping

Pour cold milk into bowl. Add pudding mix. With electric mixer at low speed, beat until well blended, 1 to 2 minutes. Fold in whipped topping. Pour into shallow pan and freeze until firm, about 4 hours.

FAST AND FABULOUS FRUIT

Makes 3 cups or 6 servings

1 **package (4-serving size) JELL-O® Instant Pudding and
   Pie Filling, any flavor**
1 **can (20 ounces) crushed pineapple in juice***
1 **cup thawed COOL WHIP® Non-Dairy Whipped Topping****

Combine pudding mix and fruit with juice in bowl. With electric mixer at
low speed, beat until well blended, 1 to 2 minutes. Blend in whipped
topping. Spoon into individual dessert dishes. Garnish as desired.

*Substitution: Use 1 can (16 ounces) sliced peaches, or 1 can (17 ounces)
fruit cocktail, pitted dark sweet cherries or apricot halves, diced.

**Substitution: Use 1 cup sour cream, whipped cream cheese, cottage
cheese or plain yogurt.

EASY BUT SPECIAL

Fuss-free party fare that looks spectacular!
These irresistible creations will leave everyone
awestruck at your next get-together.
Only you need to know the little tricks that make
them a breeze to prepare.

Peachy Orange Ring

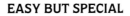

PEACHY ORANGE RING

Makes about 5¼ cups or 10 servings

1 can (16 ounces) sliced peaches, drained
2 packages (4-serving size) or 1 package (8-serving size)
    JELL-O® Brand Orange Flavor Gelatin
2 cups boiling water
1½ cups cold water or ginger ale
½ cup chopped celery
½ cup chopped pecans

Set aside 7 peach slices; dice remaining peaches. Dissolve gelatin in boiling water. Add cold water. Measure 1¼ cups of the gelatin and pour into 6-cup fluted tube pan. Chill until set but not firm. Chill remaining gelatin until thickened. Arrange peach slices on set gelatin in pan. Gently press peaches down almost to the bottom of the pan. Chill. Add diced peaches, celery and nuts to thickened gelatin; spoon over set gelatin in pan. Chill until firm, about 4 hours. Unmold. Garnish with endive and additional peach slices, if desired.

LEMON-CHEESE CHIFFON

Makes 2½ cups or 5 servings

¾ cup boiling water
1 package (4-serving size) JELL-O® Brand Lemon Flavor
    Gelatin
1 tablespoon sugar
½ cup cold water
    Ice cubes
1 package (3 ounces) cream cheese, softened and cut up

Pour boiling water into blender. Add gelatin and sugar. Cover and blend at low speed until gelatin is completely dissolved, about 30 seconds. Combine cold water and ice cubes to make 1¼ cups. Add to gelatin and stir until ice is partially melted. Then add cream cheese. Blend at high speed for 1 minute. Pour into individual dessert dishes or serving bowl. Chill until set, about 1 hour. Garnish as desired.

— ■ —

LAYERED PEACH SALAD

Makes about 4 cups or 8 servings

1 can (8 ounces) sliced peaches, drained
¼ cup sliced celery
¾ cup boiling water
1 package (4-serving size) JELL-O® Brand Gelatin, any red
    flavor
½ cup cold water
    Ice cubes

Arrange peach slices and celery in 8×4-inch loaf pan. Pour boiling water into blender. Add gelatin. Cover and blend at low speed until gelatin is completely dissolved, about 30 seconds. Combine cold water and ice cubes to make 1 cup. Add to gelatin and stir until ice is partially melted; then

CONTINUED

blend at high speed for 30 seconds. Pour into pan. Chill until firm, about 3 hours. Salad layers as it chills. Unmold. Garnish with celery leaves and additional peach slices, if desired.

Layered Pear-Cucumber Salad: Prepare Layered Peach Salad as directed, substituting 1 can (8½ ounces) pear halves, drained and sliced, ¼ cup shredded peeled cucumber and lime or lemon flavor gelatin for peaches, celery and red flavor gelatin. Garnish with parsley and additional pear slices, if desired.

Layered Carrot-Pineapple Salad: Prepare Layered Peach Salad as directed, substituting 1 can (8¼ ounces) pineapple slices, drained and cut in half, ¼ cup shredded carrot and orange flavor gelatin for the peaches, celery and red flavor gelatin. Garnish with chicory and carrot curls, if desired.

Layered Grapefruit-Cabbage Salad: Prepare Layered Peach Salad as directed, substituting ¾ cup grapefruit sections, ¼ cup shredded cabbage and strawberry flavor gelatin for the peaches, celery and red flavor gelatin. Garnish with endive and additional grapefruit sections, if desired.

STRAWBERRY-BANANA PIE

Makes one 9-inch pie

1 medium banana, sliced
1 prepared 9-inch graham cracker crumb crust, cooled
1 package (4-serving size) JELL-O® Brand Strawberry-
     Banana Flavor Gelatin
⅔ cup boiling water
½ cup cold water
    Ice cubes
3½ cups (8 ounces) COOL WHIP® Non-Dairy Whipped
     Topping, thawed
1 cup sliced strawberries

Arrange banana slices in bottom of crust. Completely dissolve gelatin in boiling water. Combine cold water and ice cubes to make 1¼ cups. Add to gelatin, stirring until slightly thickened. Remove any unmelted ice. Using wire whisk, blend in whipped topping; then whip until smooth. Fold in strawberries. Chill until mixture mounds. Spoon over banana in pie crust. Chill about 2 hours. Garnish with additional strawberries and banana slices, if desired.

— ■ —

MINTED PEAR PIE

Makes one 9-inch pie

1 package (4-serving size) JELL-O® Brand Lime Flavor
Gelatin

⅔ cup boiling water

2 teaspoons finely chopped fresh mint or 1 teaspoon dried
mint leaves, crumbled

½ cup cold water
Ice cubes

3½ cups (8 ounces) COOL WHIP® Non-Dairy Whipped
Topping, thawed

1½ cups coarsely chopped peeled fresh pears

1 prepared 9-inch chocolate cookie crumb crust, cooled

Completely dissolve gelatin in boiling water; add mint. Combine cold water
and ice cubes to make 1¼ cups. Add to gelatin, stirring until slightly
thickened. Remove any unmelted ice. Using wire whisk, blend in whipped
topping; then whip until smooth. Fold in pears. Chill until mixture mounds.
Spoon into pie crust. Chill about 2 hours. Garnish with chocolate curls or
mint sprigs, if desired.

QUICK FLUFFY FROSTING

Makes about 3 cups

1½ cups cold milk

1 envelope DREAM WHIP® Whipped Topping Mix

1 package (4-serving size) JELL-O® Instant Pudding and
Pie Filling, any flavor

Pour milk into deep narrow bowl; add whipped topping mix and pudding
mix. With electric mixer at low speed, beat until well blended. Gradually
increase beating speed to high and whip until mixture forms soft peaks, 4
to 6 minutes. Makes enough to frost 2-layer 9-inch cake. Store frosted
cake in refrigerator.

*Top to bottom: Strawberry-Banana Pie (see page 75),
Pineapple-Coconut Pie (see page 78), Minted Pear Pie ▶*

— ■ —

PINEAPPLE-COCONUT PIE

Makes one 9-inch pie

1 package (4-serving size) JELL-O® Brand Orange Flavor
  Gelatin
⅔ cup boiling water
¼ cup rum or 1½ teaspoons rum extract
½ cup cold water
  Ice cubes
3½ cups (8 ounces) COOL WHIP® Non-Dairy Whipped
  Topping, thawed
1 can (8¼ ounces) crushed pineapple, drained
½ cup BAKER'S® ANGEL FLAKE® Coconut
1 prepared 9-inch graham cracker crumb crust, cooled

Completely dissolve gelatin in boiling water. Stir in rum. Combine cold water and ice cubes to make 1¼ cups. Add to gelatin, stirring until slightly thickened. Remove any unmelted ice. Using wire whisk, blend in whipped topping; then whip until smooth. Fold in pineapple and coconut. Chill until mixture mounds. Spoon into pie crust. Chill about 2 hours. Garnish with pineapple chunks and additional coconut, if desired.

SOUR CREAM RASPBERRY PUDDING

Makes 2½ cups or 4 servings

¼ cup raspberry preserves
1½ cups cold milk
½ cup sour cream
1 package (4-serving size) JELL-O® Vanilla Flavor Instant
  Pudding and Pie Filling

Spread preserves in bottom of serving bowl or place 1 tablespoon in each dessert dish. Combine milk and sour cream in mixing bowl. Add pudding mix. With electric mixer at low speed, beat until blended, about 1 minute. Pour over preserves. Let stand to set, about 5 minutes. Garnish with whipped topping and additional preserves, if desired.

FRUIT WHIP

Makes 4½ cups or 6 servings

¾ cup boiling water
1 package (4-serving size) JELL-O® Brand Gelatin, any
   flavor
½ cup cold water or fruit juice
   Ice cubes
1 cup fresh or canned fruit (optional)

Pour boiling water into blender. Add gelatin. Cover and blend at low speed until gelatin is completely dissolved, about 30 seconds. Combine cold water and ice cubes to make 1¼ cups. Add to gelatin and stir until ice is partially melted; then blend at high speed for 30 seconds. Pour into dessert glasses or serving bowl. Spoon in fruit. Chill until firm, 20 to 30 minutes. Dessert layers as it chills. Garnish with additional fruit and mint, if desired.

GELATIN JEWEL

Makes 2 cups or 4 servings

1 package (4-serving size) JELL-O® Brand Gelatin, any
     flavor
1 cup boiling water
1 cup cold water
    COOL WHIP® Non-Dairy Whipped Topping, thawed

Dissolve gelatin in boiling water. Add cold water. Pour into individual
dessert glasses. Chill until firm, about 2 hours. Make scalloped border
around outside edge of gelatin by scooping out spoonfuls with ½-teaspoon
measure. Reserve gelatin pieces to use with fruit for another dessert.
Spoon whipped topping over gelatin in glasses.

— ■ —

—■—

PUDDING PEACH SHORTCAKE

Makes 4 servings

1 cup cold milk
1 cup (½ pint) sour cream
⅛ teaspoon almond extract
1 package (4-serving size) JELL-O® Vanilla Flavor Instant
    Pudding and Pie Filling
8 thin slices pound cake
1½ cups sliced pitted peeled peaches

Combine cold milk, sour cream and almond extract in bowl. Add pudding mix. With electric mixer at low speed, beat until well blended, 1 to 2 minutes. Let stand 5 minutes. Place a slice of pound cake in each of 4 dessert dishes. Spoon ¼ cup of the pudding onto each slice. Top with half of the peaches. Repeat layers with remaining ingredients. Garnish with whipped topping, if desired.

ORANGE-GINGER DESSERT

Makes 3½ cups or 6 servings

1 package (4-serving size) JELL-O® Brand Orange or
    Orange-Pineapple Flavor Gelatin
1 cup boiling water
¾ cup chilled ginger ale
1 cup miniature marshmallows
1 cup drained orange sections or 1 can (11 ounces)
    mandarin orange sections, drained

Dissolve gelatin in boiling water. Add ginger ale. Chill until very thick. Stir in marshmallows and orange sections. Pour into 4-cup ring mold or individual molds. Chill until firm, about 3 hours. Unmold.

—■—

GLAZED PEACH CREME

Makes 5 cups or 10 servings

2 packages (4-serving size) or 1 package (8-serving size)
  JELL-O® Brand Peach, Orange, Raspberry or Black
  Cherry Flavor Gelatin

2 cups boiling water

¾ cup cold water

2 cups (1 pint) vanilla ice cream

1 can (8¾ ounces) sliced peaches, drained, or 1 sliced
  peeled fresh peach

Completely dissolve gelatin in boiling water. Measure 1 cup of the gelatin; add cold water. Chill until slightly thickened.

Add ice cream to remaining gelatin; stir until melted and smooth. Pour ice cream mixture into serving bowl or individual dessert glasses. Chill until set but not firm. Arrange peach slices on ice cream layer in bowl. Spoon clear gelatin over peaches. Chill until set, about 4 hours.

CHOCOLATE RASPBERRY ICE CREAM PIE

Makes one 9-inch pie

1 package (4-serving size) JELL-O® Brand Raspberry
 Flavor Gelatin

⅔ cup boiling water

1 cup (½ pint) vanilla ice cream

2 cups thawed COOL WHIP® Non-Dairy Whipped Topping

1 cup fresh raspberries

1 prepared 9-inch chocolate cookie crumb crust, cooled

Completely dissolve gelatin in boiling water. Add ice cream by spoonfuls, stirring until melted and smooth. Blend in whipped topping and raspberries. Chill, if necessary, until mixture mounds. Spoon into crust. Chill about 3 hours or freeze until firm. Garnish with chocolate curls and additional whipped topping and fruit, if desired.

— ■ —

PUDDING IN A CLOUD

Makes about 3½ cups or 6 servings

1 package (4-serving size) JELL-O® Pudding and Pie Filling,
    any flavor except Lemon
2 cups milk
2 cups thawed COOL WHIP® Non-Dairy Whipped Topping

Combine pudding mix and milk in medium saucepan; blend well. Cook and stir over medium heat until mixture comes to a full boil. Pour into bowl; cover surface of pudding with plastic wrap. Chill.

Spoon ⅓ cup of the whipped topping into each of 6 dessert glasses. Using the back of a spoon, make a depression in the center and spread topping up the sides of each glass. Spoon pudding mixture into glasses. Chill.

QUICK COFFEE FLUFF

Makes 8 or 9 servings

1 tablespoon MAXWELL HOUSE® or YUBAN®
    Instant Coffee
2¼ cups cold milk
1 envelope DREAM WHIP® Whipped Topping Mix
1 package (6-serving size) JELL-O® Vanilla Flavor Instant
    Pudding and Pie Filling
½ teaspoon cinnamon (optional)
½ cup chopped nuts (optional)

Dissolve coffee in milk in bowl. Add whipped topping mix, pudding mix and cinnamon. With electric mixer at low speed, beat until well blended, about 1 minute. Gradually increase beating speed and beat until mixture forms soft peaks, 3 to 6 minutes. Fold in nuts. Spoon into individual dessert glasses. Chill. Garnish with additional whipped topping and pecan halves.

Clockwise from top: Pudding Tart-in-a-Dish (see page 86),
◄ *Quick Coffee Fluff, Pudding in a Cloud*

— ■ —

— ■ —

PUDDING TART-IN-A-DISH

Makes about 2½ cups or 4 servings

1 package (4-serving size) JELL-O® Pudding and Pie Filling,
   any flavor except Lemon
2 cups milk
½ cup graham cracker crumbs or cookie crumbs
2 to 3 teaspoons butter or margarine, melted

Combine pudding mix and milk in medium saucepan; blend well. Cook and stir over medium heat until mixture comes to a full boil. Cool 5 minutes, stirring twice.

Combine crumbs and butter; mix well. Press mixture on bottom and sides of individual dessert glasses. Spoon pudding into crumb-lined glasses. Chill. Garnish with prepared whipped topping and additional crumbs, if desired.

PUDDING POKE CAKE

Makes one 13×9-inch cake

1 package (2-layer size) yellow cake mix or pudding-
   included cake mix*
   Ingredients for cake mix
2 packages (4-serving size) JELL-O® Chocolate Flavor
   Instant Pudding and Pie Filling*
1 cup confectioners sugar
4 cups cold milk

Prepare and bake cake mix as directed on package for 13×9-inch cake. Remove from oven. Poke holes at once down through cake to pan with round handle of wooden spoon. (Or poke holes with plastic drinking straw, using turning motion to make large holes.) Holes should be at 1-inch intervals.

Only after the holes are made, combine pudding mix with sugar in large bowl. Gradually stir in milk. Beat with electric mixer at low speed for not more than 1 minute. Do not overbeat. Quickly, before pudding thickens, pour about half of the thin pudding evenly over warm cake and into holes.

CONTINUED

— ■ —

(This will make stripes in cake.) Allow remaining pudding to thicken slightly; then spoon over the top, swirling it to "frost" the cake. Chill at least 1 hour. Store cake in refrigerator.

Peanut Butter Poke Cake: Prepare Pudding Poke Cake as directed, using chocolate flavor instant pudding and pie filling. Add ½ cup peanut butter to pudding mix and confectioners sugar with ½ cup of the milk; blend well before adding remaining milk and beating.

*Additional Flavor Combinations
Use yellow cake mix with butterscotch or pistachio flavor pudding mix.

Use chocolate cake mix with chocolate, vanilla, coconut cream, banana cream or pistachio flavor pudding mix.

Use lemon cake mix with lemon flavor pudding mix.

Use white cake mix with butterscotch, chocolate, pistachio or vanilla pudding mix.

Fruited Tilt

EASY BUT SPECIAL

QUICK CHOCOLATE LOAF

Makes about 3⅓ cups or 6 servings

1½ cups cold milk
1 envelope DREAM WHIP® Whipped Topping Mix
1 package (4-serving size) JELL-O® Chocolate or Chocolate
  Fudge Instant Pudding and Pie Filling
12 ladyfingers, split*

Pour cold milk into bowl. Add whipped topping mix and pudding mix. With electric mixer at low speed, beat until well blended, about 1 minute. Gradually increase beating speed and beat until mixture forms soft peaks, 3 to 6 minutes.

Line 8×4-inch loaf pan with waxed paper. Then line bottom and sides of pan with split ladyfingers; trim tops of ladyfingers, if necessary. Spoon in pudding mixture. Chill or freeze until firm, about 4 hours. Invert onto serving plate, remove paper and cut in slices.

*Substitution: Use 8-ounce pound cake, thinly sliced and cut into strips.

FRUITED TILT

Makes 6 to 8 servings

1 package (4-serving size) JELL-O® Brand Gelatin, any
  flavor
¾ cup boiling water
½ cup cold water
  Ice cubes
1 cup sliced or diced fresh fruit*
1 cup thawed COOL WHIP® Non-Dairy Whipped Topping

Dissolve gelatin in boiling water. Combine cold water and ice cubes to make 1¼ cups. Add to gelatin, stirring until slightly thickened. Remove any unmelted ice. Fold in fruit. Spoon half of the fruited gelatin into individual parfait glasses. Tilt glasses in refrigerator by catching bases between bars of rack and leaning tops against wall; chill until set. Spoon whipped topping into glasses; top with remaining fruited gelatin. Stand glasses upright. Chill about 30 minutes.

*Do not use fresh pineapple, kiwifruit, mango, papaya or figs.

— ■ —

GELATIN CUTOUTS

Makes about 9 cutouts

1 package (4-serving size) JELL-O® Brand Gelatin, any
    flavor
1½ cups boiling water

Completely dissolve gelatin in boiling water. Pour into 8- or 9-inch pan to
depth of ½ inch. (For shallower cutouts use 13×9-inch pan.) Chill until
firm, about 4 hours. Cut firm gelatin with 2½-inch cookie cutters that
have been dipped in warm water. Carefully transfer cutouts to serving
plates, using broad spatula that has been dipped in warm water. Or serve
on pudding or gelatin squares, if desired. Flake remaining gelatin with fork
and use for another dessert with fruit or whipped topping.

Note: Firm gelatin may be unmolded onto tray before cutting.

— ■ —

SELF-LAYERING DESSERT

Makes 3 cups or 6 servings

¾ cup boiling water
1 package (4-serving size) JELL-O® Brand Gelatin, any
  flavor
½ cup cold water
  Ice cubes
½ cup thawed COOL WHIP® Non-Dairy Whipped Topping

Pour boiling water into blender. Add gelatin. Cover and blend at low speed until gelatin is completely dissolved, about 30 seconds. Combine cold water and ice cubes to make 1¼ cups. Add to gelatin and stir until ice is partially melted. Then add whipped topping; blend at high speed for 30 seconds. Pour into dessert glasses. Chill about 30 minutes. Dessert layers as it chills. Garnish as desired.

— ■ —

LAYERED FRUIT SALAD

Makes about 5½ cups or 10 servings

  2 **packages (4-serving size) or 1 package (8-serving size) JELL-O® Brand Orange or Wild Strawberry Flavor Gelatin**

1½ **cups boiling water**

  1 **cup cold water**
    Ice cubes

  2 **tablespoons lemon juice**

  2 **cups fresh fruit (banana slices, orange sections and halved seedless grapes)**

  1 **package (3 ounces) cream cheese, softened**

⅛ **teaspoon cinnamon**

Completely dissolve gelatin in boiling water. Combine cold water and ice cubes to make 2½ cups. Add to gelatin with lemon juice, stirring until slightly thickened. Remove any unmelted ice. Measure 1 cup of the gelatin; set aside. Stir fruit into remaining gelatin; pour into serving bowl. Place measured gelatin, cheese and cinnamon in blender. Cover and blend until smooth. Spoon carefully over gelatin mixture in bowl. Chill until set, about 2 hours. Garnish with lettuce and additional fruit, if desired.

— ■ —

CHERRY CHEESE MOLD

Makes 4 cups or 8 servings

1 can (8 ounces) dark sweet pitted cherries
1 package (4-serving size) JELL-O® Brand Cherry Flavor
  Gelatin
1½ cups crushed ice
2 packages (3 ounces each) cream cheese, softened and
  cut up

Drain cherries, reserving syrup. Add water to syrup to make ¾ cup. Pour into small saucepan. Bring to a boil over high heat. Pour boiling liquid into blender. Add gelatin. Cover and blend at low speed until gelatin is completely dissolved, about 30 seconds. Add crushed ice and cream cheese. Blend at high speed for 1 minute. Pour into 4-cup mold or bowl or individual dessert dishes. Drop cherries into gelatin mixture, one at a time. Chill until firm, about 1 hour. Unmold.

ORANGE COCONUT CREAM PUDDING

Makes 4 servings

1 package (4-serving size) JELL-O® Coconut Cream,
  Vanilla, Chocolate or Chocolate Fudge Flavor Pudding
  and Pie Filling
1½ cups milk
½ cup orange juice
½ teaspoon grated orange rind

Microwave:* Combine pudding mix and milk in 1½-quart microwave-safe bowl; blend well. Cook at HIGH 3 minutes. Stir well and cook 2 minutes longer; then stir again and cook 1 minute or until mixture comes to a boil. Stir in orange juice and rind. Spoon into individual dessert dishes. Chill.

*Ovens vary. Cooking time is approximate.

CHERRY-VANILLA PARFAIT

Makes 6 servings

1 cup cold milk

1 cup (½ pint) sour cream

¼ teaspoon almond extract

1 package (4-serving size) JELL-O® Vanilla or French
  Vanilla Flavor Instant Pudding and Pie Filling

1 cup canned cherry pie filling

Combine cold milk, sour cream and almond extract in bowl. Add pudding mix. With electric mixer at low speed, beat until well blended, 1 to 2 minutes. Layer pudding and cherry pie filling in individual parfait glasses. Chill about 1 hour.

MOCK DEVONSHIRE CREAM

Makes 4 cups or 8 servings

1 package (4-serving size) JELL-O® Vanilla or French
  Vanilla Flavor Pudding and Pie Filling

3 cups half and half

2 packages (3 ounces each) cream cheese, softened and
  cut up

  Sweetened fresh strawberries, raspberries, blueberries
  or peaches*

Combine pudding mix and half and half in medium saucepan; blend well. Cook and stir over medium heat until mixture comes to a full boil. Remove from heat. Pour into bowl. Blend in cream cheese with fork until mixture has small lumps of cheese throughout. Cover and chill. Serve with fruit.

*Substitution: Use 1 package (10 ounces) BIRDS EYE® Quick Thaw Fruits, any variety; thaw just before serving.

Cherry-Vanilla Parfait ▶

LAYERED PUDDING

Makes about 2½ cups or 4 servings

1½ **cups cold milk**
  1 **package (4-serving size) JELL-O® Instant Pudding and Pie Filling, any flavor**
  1 **cup thawed COOL WHIP® Non-Dairy Whipped Topping**

Pour cold milk into bowl. Add pudding mix. With electric mixer at low speed, beat for 1 minute. Spoon ¼ cup of the pudding into each of 4 dessert glasses. Fold whipped topping into remaining pudding. Spoon over plain pudding in glasses. Garnish with additional whipped topping and chocolate curls, if desired.

Three Layer Pudding: Prepare Layered Pudding as directed, increasing whipped topping to 1¾ cups. Fold 1 cup of the whipped topping into ½ cup of the pudding; layer with remaining plain pudding and remaining whipped topping in 6 parfait glasses. Makes about 3½ cups or 6 servings.

ORANGE AND GRAPEFRUIT BOWL

Makes about 8 cups or 12 servings

1 cup fresh orange sections, halved

1 cup fresh grapefruit sections, halved

2 tablespoons sugar

2 packages (4-serving size) or 1 package (8-serving size)
   JELL-O® Brand Orange or Lemon Flavor Gelatin

2 cups boiling water

Sprinkle fruit with sugar; let stand 10 to 15 minutes. Drain, reserving liquid. Add water to liquid to make 1½ cups. Dissolve gelatin in boiling water. Add measured liquid. Measure 1½ cups of the gelatin; set aside. Chill remaining gelatin until slightly thickened. Fold in drained fruit. Pour into 8-cup serving bowl. Chill until set but not firm.

Chill measured gelatin until slightly thickened. With electric mixer at medium speed, beat until fluffy, thick and about doubled in volume. Gently spoon over fruited gelatin in bowl. Chill until firm, about 4 hours. Garnish with additional fruit and mint leaves, if desired.

— ■ —

SUPER SNACKS

If you're tired of the same old between-meal
nibbles, then super snacks are for you!
These delectable munchies are quick to make
and are ideal for after-school treats and
late-night refrigerator raids.

Peanut Butter Snacking Cups

PEANUT BUTTER SNACKING CUPS

Makes 12 servings

3/4 cup graham cracker crumbs

3 tablespoons butter or margarine, melted

3½ cups (8 ounces) COOL WHIP® Non-Dairy Whipped
    Topping, thawed

1 cup milk

½ cup chunky peanut butter

1 package (4-serving size) JELL-O® Vanilla Flavor Instant
    Pudding and Pie Filling

¼ cup strawberry preserves

Line 12-cup muffin pan with paper baking cups. Combine crumbs and butter; mix well. Press about 1 tablespoon of the crumb mixture into each cup. Top each with about 1 tablespoon of the whipped topping. Gradually add milk to peanut butter in bowl, blending until smooth. Add pudding mix. With electric mixer at low speed, beat until blended, 1 to 2 minutes. Fold in remaining whipped topping. Spoon into crumb-lined cups. Top each cup with 1 teaspoon of the preserves. Freeze about 4 hours. To serve, peel off papers.

FLUFFY ICE CREAM DESSERT

Makes 2½ cups or 5 servings

1 cup sliced or diced fresh fruit*

3/4 cup boiling water

1 package (4-serving size) JELL-O® Brand Gelatin, any
    flavor

½ cup ice cubes

1 cup (½ pint) vanilla ice cream

Spoon fruit into individual dessert dishes. Pour boiling water into blender. Add gelatin. Cover and blend at low speed until gelatin is completely dissolved, about 30 seconds. Add ice cubes and stir until ice is partially melted. Add ice cream and blend at high speed for 30 seconds. Pour mixture over fruit in dessert dishes. Chill until soft-set, 5 minutes.

*Do not use fresh pineapple, kiwifruit, mango, papaya or figs.

EASY PUDDING MILK SHAKE

Makes about 5 cups or 4 to 6 servings

3 cups cold milk

1 package (4-serving size) JELL-O® Instant Pudding and
   Pie Filling, any flavor

3 scoops (about 1½ cups) ice cream, any flavor

Pour cold milk into blender. Add pudding mix and ice cream. Cover and blend at high speed for 15 seconds or until smooth. Serve at once. Mixture thickens as it stands; thin with additional milk, if desired.

Note: To prepare single serving, use 1 cup milk, 2½ to 3 tablespoons (¼ package) instant pudding and pie filling and 1 scoop ice cream. If desired, combine in 1-quart jar; cover and shake well.

CHOCOLATE CHEESE SQUARES

Makes 9 servings

⅓ cup butter or margarine

1¼ cups graham cracker crumbs

¼ cup plus 3 tablespoons sugar

2 packages (4-serving size) JELL-O® Chocolate Flavor
   Pudding and Pie Filling

3½ cups milk

2 packages (8 ounces each) cream cheese, softened and
   cut up

1 teaspoon vanilla

Microwave:* Melt butter in 8-inch microwave-safe square baking dish at HIGH for 30 seconds. Add crumbs and 3 tablespoons of the sugar; mix well. Press firmly onto bottom of dish. Cook 1½ minutes. Cool.

Combine pudding mix, milk and remaining sugar in 2½-quart microwave-safe bowl. Cook at HIGH for 4 minutes. Stir well and cook 2 minutes longer; then stir again and cook 2 minutes or until mixture comes to a boil. Add cream cheese and vanilla. Stir until smooth. Pour over crumb mixture in pan. Chill about 3 hours. Cut into squares.

*Ovens vary. Cooking time is approximate.

Easy Pudding Milk Shake ▶

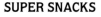

CHERRY WALDORF SNACK

Makes 2½ cups or 5 servings

 1 **package (4-serving size) JELL-O® Brand Cherry Flavor Gelatin**
    Dash salt
 ¾ **cup boiling water or apple juice**
 ½ **cup cold water or apple juice**
    Ice cubes
 ½ **cup diced peeled pear or apple**
 1 **small banana, sliced or diced**
 ¼ **cup sliced celery or chopped nuts**

Completely dissolve gelatin and salt in boiling water. Combine cold water and ice cubes to make 1¼ cups. Add to gelatin, stirring until slightly thickened. Remove any unmelted ice. Fold in fruits and celery. Spoon into bowl or individual dishes. Chill until set, about 2 hours. Garnish with additional fresh fruit and celery leaves, if desired.

FRUIT CREAM CHEESE DESSERT

Makes about 4 cups or 8 servings

1 cup boiling water
1 package (4-serving size) JELL-O® Brand Gelatin, any
    flavor
¾ cup cold water
1 package (3 ounces) cream cheese, softened and cut up
1 cup thawed COOL WHIP® Non-Dairy Whipped Topping
2 cups mixed fresh fruit*

Pour boiling water in blender. Add gelatin. Cover and blend at low speed until gelatin is completely dissolved, about 30 seconds. Add cold water and cream cheese. Blend at high speed until smooth, about 30 seconds. Chill until thickened. Fold in whipped topping. Arrange fruit in bowl or individual dessert dishes. Top with creamy mixture. Chill until set, about 1 hour.

*Do not use fresh pineapple, kiwifruit, mango, papaya or figs.

PUDDING TORTONI

Makes 3½ cups or 6 servings

1¼ cups cold milk
1 package (4-serving size) JELL-O® Pistachio or Vanilla
    Flavor Instant Pudding and Pie Filling
1¾ cups thawed COOL WHIP® Non-Dairy Whipped Topping
¾ cup BAKER'S® ANGEL FLAKE® Coconut, toasted*
¼ cup chopped drained maraschino cherries
½ teaspoon almond extract

Pour cold milk into bowl. Add pudding mix. With electric mixer at low speed, beat until well blended, 1 to 2 minutes. Blend in whipped topping. Fold in coconut, cherries and almond extract. Spoon into muffin pan lined with paper baking cups. Freeze until firm, about 3 hours.

*To toast coconut: Spread coconut in a thin layer in shallow pan. Toast in preheated 350° oven for 7 to 12 minutes or until lightly browned, stirring frequently.

MUFFIN PAN SNACKS

Makes 4 cups or 8 to 10 servings

1 package (4-serving size) JELL-O® Brand Lemon Flavor
  Gelatin
½ teaspoon salt
⅛ teaspoon garlic powder
1½ cups boiling water
2 teaspoons vinegar
1 teaspoon vegetable oil
⅛ teaspoon black pepper
⅛ teaspoon dried oregano, crumbled
  Snack combinations*

CONTINUED

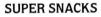
Dissolve gelatin, salt and garlic powder in boiling water. Add vinegar, oil, pepper and oregano. Place aluminum-foil baking cups in muffin pans. Place different snack combinations in each cup, filling each about ⅔ full. Then fill with gelatin mixture. Chill until firm, about 2 hours. Unmold carefully from foil cups. Serve with crisp salad greens, if desired.

*Snack Combinations

Use cauliflower florets with diced pimiento.

Use cucumber slices with tomato slices.

Use chopped hard-cooked egg with chopped cucumber and pickle.

Use shredded carrot with raisins.

Use drained canned button or sliced mushrooms with pimiento strips.

Use diced apple with chopped nuts.

Use sliced hard-cooked egg with anchovies.

Use cubed cream cheese with chopped nuts.

Use diced pimiento with diced green pepper and tomato.

Use sliced celery with sliced ripe or stuffed green olives.

APPLE-ORANGE MOLD

Makes about 6 cups or 12 servings

2 packages (4-serving size) or 1 package (8-serving size) JELL-O® Brand Strawberry Flavor Gelatin
2 cups boiling water
1½ cups cold water
1 can (11 ounces) mandarin orange sections, drained
2 cups chopped apples
½ cup chopped walnuts (optional)
¼ teaspoon cinnamon (optional)

Dissolve gelatin in boiling water. Add cold water. Measure ¾ cup of the gelatin and pour into 6-cup mold. Chill about 30 minutes. Arrange some of the orange sections on the gelatin. Chill remaining gelatin until thickened. Fold remaining orange sections, apples, walnuts and cinnamon into thickened gelatin. Spoon over orange sections in mold. Chill until firm, about 4 hours. Unmold. Serve as dessert, or garnish with crisp greens and serve as salad.

— ■ —

TOMATO AND COTTAGE CHEESE SALAD

Makes about 5½ cups or 10 servings

2 packages (4-serving size) or 1 package (8-serving size)
   JELL-O® Brand Lemon Flavor Gelatin
1½ cups boiling water
1 container (12 ounces) small curd cottage cheese
2 tablespoons mayonnaise
1 tablespoon chopped chives
2 cups tomato juice
½ teaspoon salt
2 tablespoons lemon juice
1 tablespoon minced onion
1 tablespoon prepared horseradish

Dissolve gelatin in boiling water. Combine cottage cheese, mayonnaise and chives. Measure ⅓ cup of the gelatin and stir into cottage cheese mixture. Chill until slightly thickened.

To remaining gelatin, add tomato juice, salt, lemon juice, onion and horseradish. Pour half of the tomato mixture into 6-cup ring mold; chill until slightly thickened. Chill remaining tomato mixture. Spoon cottage cheese mixture over tomato mixture in mold. Top with remaining slightly thickened tomato mixture. Chill until set, about 4 hours. Unmold.

GLAZED POPCORN

Makes 2 quarts

8 cups popped popcorn
¼ cup butter or margarine
3 tablespoons light corn syrup
½ cup packed light brown sugar or granulated sugar
1 package (4-serving size) JELL-O® Brand Gelatin, any
   flavor

Place popcorn in large bowl. Heat butter and syrup in small saucepan over low heat. Stir in brown sugar and gelatin; bring to a boil over medium heat. Reduce heat to low and gently simmer for 5 minutes. Pour syrup immedi-

CONTINUED

— ■ —

ately over popcorn, tossing to coat well. Spread popcorn on aluminum-foil-lined 15×10×1-inch pan, using two forks to spread evenly. Bake in pre-heated 300° oven for 10 minutes. Cool. Remove from pan and break into small pieces.

Rainbow Popcorn: Prepare Glazed Popcorn 3 times, using 3 different gelatin colors, such as strawberry, lemon and lime. Bake as directed and break into pieces. Layer 3 cups of each variety in 3-quart bowl. Serve remaining popcorn at another time. Makes 6 quarts.

Rainbow Popcorn

Cottage Cheese Fruited Dessert

Makes about 4 cups or 8 servings

¾ cup cottage cheese*

¾ cup COOL WHIP® Non-Dairy Whipped Topping

1 teaspoon grated lemon rind (optional)

1 package (4-serving size) JELL-O® Brand Gelatin, any
    flavor

¾ cup boiling water

½ cup cold water
    Ice cubes

1 can (8 ounces) pineapple chunks, drained

1 medium banana, sliced

CONTINUED

Combine cottage cheese, whipped topping and rind; spoon into individual dessert glasses or serving bowl. Chill. Completely dissolve gelatin in boiling water. Combine cold water and ice cubes to make 1¼ cups. Add to gelatin, stirring until slightly thickened. Remove any unmelted ice. Stir in fruit. Spoon into glasses. Chill until set, about 1 hour.

*Substitution: Use ½ cup plain yogurt.

LEMON FREEZE

Makes 8 or 9 servings

1 cup graham cracker crumbs
3 tablespoons sugar
¼ cup butter or margarine, softened
2½ cups cold milk
1 teaspoon grated lemon rind
¼ cup lemon juice
1 package (6-serving size) JELL-O® Lemon Flavor Instant Pudding and Pie Filling
2 cups thawed COOL WHIP® Non-Dairy Whipped Topping

Combine crumbs, sugar and butter; mix well. Press firmly on bottom of 9-inch square pan, reserving 2 tablespoons of the crumb mixture for garnish, if desired. Bake in preheated 375° oven for about 8 minutes. Cool thoroughly on wire rack.

Pour cold milk into bowl. Add lemon rind, lemon juice and pudding mix. With electric mixer at low speed, beat until well blended, 1 to 2 minutes. Blend in whipped topping. Pour immediately into crust. Sprinkle with reserved crumbs. Freeze until firm, about 4 hours. Remove pan from freezer about 30 minutes before serving.

ICE CREAM WITH HOT CHOCOLATE PUDDING

Makes 6 to 8 servings

> 1 package (4-serving size) JELL-O® Chocolate Flavor
>   Pudding and Pie Filling*
> 2 cups milk
> 2 cups (1 pint) vanilla or chocolate ice cream*

Combine pudding mix and milk in medium saucepan; blend well. Cook and stir over medium heat until mixture comes to a full boil. Scoop ice cream into individual dessert dishes. Immediately pour hot pudding over ice cream in dishes. Serve at once.

Note: For fewer servings, pour any remaining pudding into individual serving dishes and chill.

*Additional Flavor Combinations
Use vanilla flavor pudding mix with chocolate ice cream.

Use butterscotch flavor pudding mix with chocolate or vanilla ice cream.

Use coconut cream flavor pudding mix with vanilla ice cream.

Use banana cream flavor pudding mix with chocolate or vanilla ice cream.

FROZEN PUDDING

Makes 2⅓ cups or 4 servings

> 1 cup cold milk
> 1 cup cold heavy cream or milk
> 1 package (4-serving size) JELL-O® Instant Pudding and
>   Pie Filling, any flavor*
> 1 to 2 tablespoons sugar*

Pour cold milk and cold heavy cream into bowl. Add pudding mix and sugar. With electric mixer at low speed, beat until just blended, about 1 minute. Pour into shallow pan and freeze until firm, about 4 hours. Let stand at room temperature 15 minutes before serving.

Note: Mixture may also be poured into 8×4-inch loaf pan and frozen until firm, about 6 hours. Unmold and slice to serve.

*With coconut cream flavor instant pudding and pie filling, omit sugar.

Ice Cream with Hot Chocolate Pudding

GARDEN SALAD

Makes 3 cups or 6 servings

1 medium tomato, seeded and chopped (about 1 cup)
½ cup diced seeded peeled cucumber
¼ cup chopped green pepper
2 scallions, sliced
2 tablespoons vinegar
¼ teaspoon salt
   Dash black pepper
1 package (4-serving size) JELL-O® Brand Lemon Flavor Gelatin
¾ cup boiling water
½ cup cold water
   Ice cubes

Combine vegetables, vinegar, salt and pepper; set aside. Completely dissolve gelatin in boiling water. Combine cold water and ice cubes to make 1¼ cups. Add to gelatin, stirring until slightly thickened. Remove any unmelted ice. Stir in vegetable mixture. Chill until thickened, about 5 minutes. Pour into individual dishes. Chill until set, about 30 minutes. Garnish with additional fresh vegetables, if desired.

TOMATO ASPIC

Makes about 2 cups or 4 servings

1 package (4-serving size) JELL-O® Brand Lemon or Orange Flavor Gelatin
1 cup boiling tomato juice or vegetable juice cocktail
⅔ cup cold tomato juice or vegetable juice cocktail
1 tablespoon lemon juice
1 to 2 teaspoons prepared horseradish
½ teaspoon onion powder (optional)

Dissolve gelatin in boiling tomato juice. Add cold tomato juice, lemon juice, horseradish and onion powder. Pour into 9×5- or 8×4-inch pan or 2-cup mold. Chill until firm, about 4 hours. Cut into 1-inch cubes and serve as a snack with celery stalks, or serve on tossed salad, if desired.

GELATIN ICE CREAM DESSERT

Makes 3 cups or 6 servings

1 package (4-serving size) JELL-O® Brand Gelatin, any
   flavor
1 cup boiling water
2 cups (1 pint) ice cream, any flavor

Completely dissolve gelatin in boiling water. Add ice cream by spoonfuls, stirring until ice cream is melted. Pour into individual dessert glasses or serving bowl. Chill until set, about 30 minutes. Garnish with fresh fruit, if desired.

FRUIT JUICE CUBES

Makes 4 servings

1 package (4-serving size) JELL-O® Brand Gelatin, any
   flavor
¾ cup boiling water
1 cup apple, orange, grape, grapefruit or canned pineapple
   juice

Dissolve gelatin in boiling water. Add fruit juice. Pour into 8- or 9-inch
square pan. Chill until firm, about 3 hours. Then cut into cubes, using
sharp knife that has been dipped in hot water. Serve with fruit or on
lettuce, if desired.

Note: For thicker cubes, use 8×4-inch or 9×5-inch loaf pan or double
recipe and use 8- or 9-inch square pan.

APPLE CIDER DESSERT

Makes 2¾ cups or 5 servings

1 **package (4-serving size) JELL-O® Brand Sugar Free Gelatin, any flavor**
¾ **cup boiling water**
½ **cup cold apple cider or juice**
    Ice cubes
1 **medium unpeeled apple, cut into matchstick pieces (about 1½ cups)**

Completely dissolve gelatin in boiling water. Combine cold cider and ice cubes to make 1¼ cups. Add to gelatin, stirring until slightly thickened. Remove any unmelted ice. Stir in apple. Pour into serving bowl or dessert dishes. Chill until set, about 1 hour. Garnish with apple slices brushed with lemon juice, if desired.

LIGHT AND EASY

Looking for something light-as-a-feather
to top off that delicious dinner or to serve as an
anytime snack? Prepare one of these
heavenly desserts, snacks or salads in a snap!
They're satisfying, but never filling.

Strawberry-Banana Snack

STRAWBERRY-BANANA SNACK

Makes about 2¾ cups or 4 or 5 servings

1 package (4-serving size) JELL-O® Brand Strawberry
   Flavor Gelatin
¾ cup boiling water
½ cup cold water
   Ice cubes
1 medium banana, sliced
   Mixed fresh fruit, sliced or diced

Completely dissolve gelatin in boiling water. Combine cold water and ice cubes to make 1¼ cups. Add to gelatin, stirring until slightly thickened. Remove any unmelted ice. Let stand until thickened, 5 to 10 minutes. Stir in banana and pour into serving bowl. Chill until set, about 1 hour. Serve topped with mixed fresh fruit.

CHAMPAGNE PEACH ICE

Makes 5⅓ cups or 10 servings

2½ cups champagne or Chablis wine
1 package (4-serving size) JELL-O® Brand Peach or Lemon
   Flavor Gelatin
¾ cup sugar
   Ice cubes
4 peaches, peeled, pitted and quartered

Pour 1 cup of the champagne in small saucepan. Bring to a boil over high heat. Completely dissolve gelatin and sugar in boiling champagne. Combine 1 cup of the remaining champagne and ice cubes to make 1¼ cups. Add to gelatin, stirring until slightly thickened.

Pour remaining ½ cup champagne in blender or food processor. Add fruit; process until pureed. Stir pureed fruit into gelatin; pour into 13×9-inch pan. Freeze until ice crystals form 1 inch around the edge, 1 to 2 hours.

Spoon half of the mixture into blender or food processor. Cover and process until smooth but not melted, about 30 seconds. Repeat procedure with remaining mixture. Spoon into chilled dessert glasses and freeze until firm, about 3 hours. Garnish with fresh peach slices brushed with lemon juice, if desired.

FRUITED CHIFFON PARFAITS

Makes 3½ cups or 7 servings

1 can (8 ounces) fruit in light syrup or juice
1 package (4-serving size) JELL-O® Brand Sugar Free
   Gelatin, any flavor
½ cup cold water
   Ice cubes
1 cup thawed COOL WHIP® Non-Dairy Whipped Topping

Drain fruit, reserving liquid. Spoon fruit into parfait glasses. Add water to reserved liquid to make ¾ cup; pour into small saucepan. Bring to a boil over high heat. Pour boiling liquid into blender. Add gelatin. Cover and blend at low speed until gelatin is completely dissolved, about 30 seconds. Combine cold water and ice cubes to make 1¼ cups. Add to gelatin and stir until ice is partially melted. Then add whipped topping. Blend at high speed for 30 seconds. Pour over fruit in glasses. Chill until set, about 30 minutes. Garnish with additional fruit, if desired.

BANANA YOGURT FREEZE

Makes 4 cups or 8 servings

1½ cups cold whole or skim milk
 1 package (4-serving size) JELL-O® Vanilla Flavor Instant
    Sugar Free Pudding and Pie Filling
 1 cup (½ pint) plain yogurt
 2 medium bananas, mashed
 1 teaspoon rum extract (optional)
 1 cup thawed COOL WHIP® Non-Dairy Whipped Topping

Pour cold milk into bowl. Add pudding mix and yogurt. With electric mixer at low speed, beat until well blended, 2 minutes. Blend in bananas, rum extract and whipped topping. Pour into paper baking cups or 4-ounce paper cups, inserting wooden sticks, if desired. Freeze until firm, about 4 hours. Remove from cups and roll in toasted flaked coconut, if desired.

Note: Dessert may be frozen in 9×5-inch loaf pan. To serve, unmold and garnish with additional whipped topping, if desired.

LAYERED BANANA SALAD

Makes 4¼ cups or 8 servings

2 packages (4-serving size) or 1 package (8-serving size)
    JELL-O® Brand Lemon or Lime Flavor Sugar Free
    Gelatin
1½ cups boiling water
1 cup cold water
    Ice cubes
1 cup sliced banana (about 1 medium)
½ cup sour cream or vanilla yogurt
¼ cup diced celery
¼ cup chopped walnuts

Completely dissolve gelatin in boiling water. Combine cold water and ice cubes to make 2 cups. Add to gelatin, stirring until slightly thickened. Remove any unmelted ice. Measure 1 cup of the gelatin; set aside. Fold banana into remaining gelatin and spoon into 5-cup serving bowl. Blend sour cream into measured gelatin. Fold in celery and nuts. Spoon carefully over banana mixture in bowl. Chill until firm, about 3 hours. Garnish with additional banana slices and mint, if desired.

FRUIT SORBET

Makes about 4 cups or 8 servings

 1 package (4-serving size) JELL-O® Brand Strawberry
   Flavor Gelatin*
¾ cup boiling water
 2 pints strawberries, hulled and pureed (about 1½ cups)*
¾ cup light corn syrup or ½ cup sugar
 2 egg whites, unbeaten, or 1 whole egg, slightly beaten**

Dissolve gelatin in boiling water. Stir in strawberries, corn syrup and egg
whites. Pour into 13×9-inch pan. Freeze until partially frozen, about 2
hours. Spoon half of the mixture into blender or food processor. Cover and
process until smooth but not melted, about 30 seconds. Pour into 1½-
quart plastic container. Repeat procedure with remaining mixture. Cover
and freeze until firm, about 6 hours.

*Additional Flavor Combinations
Use peach flavor gelatin with 4 pitted peeled peaches or plums, or 1
medium cantaloupe.

Use lemon flavor gelatin with 2 or 3 sliced bananas or 3 cups diced peeled
pears.

Use raspberry flavor gelatin with 4 pitted peeled plums or 1½ cups pureed
cranberries.

Use orange flavor gelatin with 2 or 3 sliced bananas.

Use strawberry flavor gelatin with 4 pitted peeled plums.

**Use only clean eggs with no cracks in shells.

APPLESAUCE YOGURT DESSERT

Makes 2 cups or 4 servings

1 package (4-serving size) JELL-O® Brand Sugar Free
   Gelatin, any red flavor
1 cup boiling water
¾ cup chilled unsweetened applesauce
¼ teaspoon cinnamon
½ cup vanilla yogurt

Dissolve gelatin in boiling water. Measure ¾ cup of the gelatin; add apple-sauce and cinnamon. Pour into individual dessert glasses or serving bowl. Chill until set but not firm.

Chill remaining gelatin until slightly thickened. Blend in yogurt. Spoon over gelatin in glasses. Chill until set, about 2 hours. Garnish with additional yogurt and mint leaves, if desired.

CITRUS SORBET

Makes 3 cups or 6 servings

1 package (4-serving size) JELL-O® Brand Lemon, Lime or
   Orange Flavor Gelatin
1¼ cups boiling water
1 cup ice cubes
¾ cup light corn syrup or ½ cup sugar
1 tablespoon lemon, lime or orange juice
1 tablespoon lemon, lime or orange rind
2 egg whites, unbeaten, or 1 whole egg, slightly beaten*

Completely dissolve gelatin in boiling water. Add ice cubes, stirring until ice is melted. Stir in remaining ingredients. Pour into 13×9-inch pan. Freeze until partially frozen, about 2 hours.

Spoon half of the mixture into blender or food processor. Cover and process until smooth but not melted, about 30 seconds. Pour into 1½-quart plastic container. Repeat procedure with remaining mixture. Cover and freeze until firm, about 6 hours.

*Use only clean eggs with no cracks in shell.

MELON WEDGES

Makes 6 servings

- 1 cantaloupe or honeydew melon
- 1 package (4-serving size) JELL-O® Brand Apricot or
  Orange Flavor Sugar Free Gelatin
- 1 cup boiling water
- ¾ cup cold water
- 1 banana, sliced, ½ cup sliced strawberries or 1 can
  (8¼ ounces) crushed pineapple in juice, well drained

Cut melon in half lengthwise; scoop out seeds and drain well. Dissolve gelatin in boiling water. Add cold water. Chill until slightly thickened. Stir in fruit. Pour into melon halves. Chill until firm, about 3 hours. Cut in wedges. Serve with additional fresh fruit, cottage cheese and crisp greens, if desired.

Note: Chill any excess fruited gelatin in dessert dish.

ORANGE FLUFF

Makes 3 cups or 6 servings

1 can (8½ ounces) sliced peaches in juice
¾ cup boiling water
1 package (4-serving size) JELL-O® Brand Orange Flavor
   Sugar Free Gelatin
  Ice cubes
½ cup low-fat cottage cheese
¼ teaspoon almond extract (optional)

Drain peaches, reserving juice. Add water to juice to make ½ cup; set aside. Dice peaches and place in individual dessert dishes. Pour boiling water into blender. Add gelatin. Cover and blend at low speed until gelatin is completely dissolved, about 30 seconds. Combine measured liquid and ice cubes to make 1¼ cups. Add to gelatin and stir until ice is partially melted. Then add cottage cheese and extract. Blend at high speed for 30 seconds. Pour over peaches in glasses. Chill until set, about 30 minutes. Garnish as desired.

CITRUS FRAPPÉ

Makes 3 cups or 6 servings

¾ cup boiling water
1 package (4-serving size) JELL-O® Brand Lemon, Lime or
   Orange Flavor Sugar Free Gelatin*
½ cup cold water
  Ice cubes
½ cup lemon sherbet*

Pour boiling water into blender. Add gelatin. Cover and blend at low speed until gelatin is completely dissolved, about 30 seconds. Combine cold water and ice cubes to make 1¼ cups. Add to gelatin and stir until ice is partially melted. Add sherbet and blend at high speed for 30 seconds. Spoon into dessert dishes. Chill until set, about 15 minutes.

*Additional Flavor Combinations
Use lemon flavor gelatin with lime or raspberry sherbet.

Use orange flavor gelatin with orange sherbet.

PUDDING MOUSSE

Makes 2⅔ cups or 5 servings

1½ cups cold milk
1 package (4-serving size) JELL-O® Sugar Free Instant Pudding and Pie Filling, any flavor
1 cup thawed COOL WHIP® Non-Dairy Whipped Topping

Pour cold milk into bowl. Add pudding mix. With electric mixer at low speed, beat until well blended, 1 to 2 minutes. Fold in whipped topping and spoon into dessert glasses. Garnish with additional whipped topping, if desired.

Coffee Mousse: Prepare Pudding Mousse as directed, using vanilla or chocolate flavor instant pudding and pie filling and adding 2 teaspoons MAXWELL HOUSE® or YUBAN® Instant Coffee with the pudding mix.

Lemon Mousse: Prepare Pudding Mousse as directed, using vanilla flavor instant pudding and pie filling and adding 1½ teaspoons grated lemon rind with the whipped topping.

Yogurt Fluff

— ■ —

YOGURT FLUFF

Makes 2½ cups or 5 servings

¾ cup boiling water
1 package (4-serving size) JELL-O® Brand Sugar Free
   Gelatin, any flavor
½ cup cold water
   Ice cubes
1 cup (½ pint) plain yogurt
½ teaspoon vanilla

Pour boiling water into blender. Add gelatin. Cover and blend at low speed until gelatin is completely dissolved, about 30 seconds. Combine cold water and ice cubes to make 1¼ cups. Add to gelatin and stir until ice is partially melted. Then add yogurt and vanilla. Blend at high speed for 30 seconds. Pour into dessert glasses. Chill until set, about 30 minutes. Garnish as desired.

Apple-Nut Fluff: Prepare Yogurt Fluff as directed, using any red flavor sugar free gelatin and substituting ½ cup apple juice for the cold water. After blending, stir in ¾ cup diced apple and 2 tablespoons chopped pecans. Makes 3¼ cups or 6 servings.

Fruited Yogurt Fluff: Prepare Yogurt Fluff as directed, using orange flavor or any red flavor sugar free gelatin and substituting ½ cup orange juice for the cold water. After blending, stir in ¾ cup diced orange sections or fresh pear. Makes 3¼ cups or 6 servings.

Fruited Cottage Cheese Fluff: Prepare Yogurt Fluff as directed, substituting 1 cup (½ pint) low-fat cottage cheese for the yogurt and omitting the vanilla. Top dessert with 1½ cups sliced or diced fresh fruit before serving. Makes 4½ cups or 6 servings.

— ■ —

GARDEN VEGETABLE SALAD

Makes about 2 cups or 4 servings

1 package (4-serving size) JELL-O® Brand Sugar Free
    Lemon Flavor Gelatin
½ teaspoon salt
1 cup boiling water
¾ cup cold water
1 tablespoon vinegar
½ cup sliced radishes*
1 tablespoon sliced scallions*

Dissolve gelatin and salt in boiling water. Add cold water and vinegar. Chill until slightly thickened. Stir in radishes and scallions. Pour into individual molds. Chill until firm, about 3 hours. Unmold. Garnish with escarole, sliced hard-cooked eggs and whole radishes, if desired.

*Additional Vegetable Combinations
Use 1 cup shredded carrot with ½ cup diced celery and ¼ cup sliced green olives or chopped ripe olives.

Use 1 small tomato, cut into thin wedges, with ¼ cup sliced celery or radishes and ¼ cup quartered cucumber slices.

Use ¼ cup sliced celery with ¼ cup chopped green pepper and ¼ cup sliced green olives.

FLUFFY PUDDING

Makes about 3 cups or 6 servings

1 package (4-serving size) JELL-O® Vanilla or Chocolate
    Flavor Sugar Free Pudding and Pie Filling
2 cups low-fat milk
1 cup thawed COOL WHIP® Non-Dairy Whipped Topping

Combine pudding mix and milk in medium saucepan; blend well. Cook and stir over medium heat until mixture comes to a full boil. Pour into bowl; cover surface of pudding with plastic wrap. Chill. Fold whipped topping into pudding. Spoon into dessert dishes, tart shells or meringue shells. Garnish with additional whipped topping and fruit, if desired.

— ■ —

— ▦ —

MELON DESSERT

Makes 3½ cups or 6 servings

1 **package (4-serving size) JELL-O® Brand Lime, Lemon or Orange Flavor Sugar Free Gelatin**
¾ **cup boiling water**
½ **cup orange juice or water**
   Ice cubes
1 **cup melon balls**

Completely dissolve gelatin in boiling water. Combine orange juice and ice cubes to make 1¼ cups. Add to gelatin, stirring until slightly thickened. Remove any unmelted ice. Measure 1⅓ cups gelatin; fold in melon balls. Spoon into serving bowl or dessert glasses; chill until set but not firm.

With electric mixer at medium speed, whip remaining gelatin until fluffy, thick and about doubled in volume. Pour over clear gelatin in bowl. Chill until firm, about 1 hour. Garnish with additional melon balls and mint leaves, if desired.

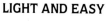

Vegetable Yogurt Salad

Makes 2½ cups or 5 servings

1 package (4-serving size) JELL-O® Brand Lemon Flavor
    Sugar Free Gelatin
1 cup boiling water
1 tablespoon vinegar
1 container (8 ounces) plain yogurt
1 cup grated carrots
½ cup chopped green pepper
1 tablespoon chopped chives

Dissolve gelatin in boiling water. Add vinegar. Chill until slightly thickened. Blend in yogurt; then fold in carrots, green pepper and chives. Pour into 2½- or 3-cup mold. Chill until firm, about 3 hours. Unmold. Garnish with celery leaves and carrot curls, if desired.

APRICOT MOUSSE

Makes 3 cups or 6 servings

¾ cup boiling water
1 package (4-serving size) JELL-O® Brand Orange Flavor
   Sugar Free Gelatin
½ cup cold water
   Ice cubes
1 cup diced fresh or canned apricots, drained
½ cup thawed COOL WHIP® Non-Dairy Whipped Topping

Pour boiling water into blender. Add gelatin. Cover and blend at low speed until gelatin is completely dissolved, about 30 seconds. Combine cold water and ice cubes to make 1¼ cups. Add to gelatin and stir until ice is partially melted. Add apricots and whipped topping. Then blend at high speed for 30 seconds or until smooth. Pour into dessert glasses. Chill until set, about 30 minutes. Garnish with additional sliced apricots, if desired.

LEMON-LIME PARFAIT

Makes 3 cups or 6 servings

¾ cup boiling water
1 package (4-serving size) JELL-O® Brand Lime Flavor
   Sugar Free Gelatin
½ cup cold water
   Ice cubes
1 teaspoon grated lemon rind
1 teaspoon grated lime rind
2 tablespoons lemon juice
1½ cups thawed COOL WHIP® Non-Dairy Whipped Topping

Pour boiling water into blender. Add gelatin. Cover and blend at low speed until gelatin is completely dissolved, about 30 seconds. Combine cold water and ice cubes to make 1¼ cups. Add to gelatin and stir until ice is partially melted. Add remaining ingredients. Blend at high speed for 30 seconds. Pour into parfait glasses. Chill until set, about 30 minutes.

CHIFFON PARFAITS

Makes 3½ cups or 7 servings

1 cup sliced fresh or thawed frozen strawberries, drained
¾ cup boiling water
1 package (4-serving size) JELL-O® Brand Strawberry
  Flavor Sugar Free Gelatin
½ cup cold water
  Ice cubes
1 cup thawed COOL WHIP® Non-Dairy Whipped Topping
½ teaspoon almond extract

Spoon strawberries into parfait glasses. Pour boiling water into blender. Add gelatin. Cover and blend at low speed until gelatin is completely dissolved, about 30 seconds. Combine cold water and ice cubes to make 1¼ cups. Add to gelatin and stir until ice is partially melted. Then add whipped topping and almond extract. Blend at high speed for 30 seconds. Pour over berries in glasses. Chill until set, about 30 minutes.

Orange Chiffon Parfaits: Prepare Chiffon Parfaits as directed, substituting 1 cup orange sections, orange flavor gelatin and 1 teaspoon grated orange rind for the strawberries, strawberry flavor gelatin and almond extract.

Raspberry Chiffon Parfaits: Prepare Chiffon Parfaits as directed, substituting 1 cup fresh raspberries and triple berry flavor gelatin for the strawberries and strawberry flavor gelatin.

SNACK CUPS

Makes about 3 cups or 6 servings

1 package (4-serving size) JELL-O® Brand Orange, Lemon
  or Lime Flavor Sugar Free Gelatin
¾ cup boiling water
½ cup cold water
  Ice cubes
1 tablespoon lemon juice (optional)
½ cup each sliced celery, chopped cabbage and shredded
  carrot*   CONTINUED

Completely dissolve gelatin in boiling water. Combine cold water and ice cubes to make 1¼ cups. Add to gelatin with lemon juice, stirring until slightly thickened. Remove any unmelted ice. Fold in vegetables; spoon into individual glasses. Chill until set, about 30 minutes. Garnish with parsley, if desired.

*Additional Vegetable Combinations
Use sliced celery with grated carrots and golden raisins.

Use sliced celery with chopped cabbage, chopped apple or sliced ripe or green pitted olives.

Use sliced celery with chopped cucumber and chopped pimiento.

Use sliced celery with drained mandarin orange sections and chopped green pepper.

PINEAPPLE SNOW

Makes about 5 cups or 6 servings

 1 package (4-serving size) JELL-O® Brand Sugar Free
     Gelatin, any flavor
 ⅛ teaspoon salt
 1 cup boiling water
 ¾ cup cold canned pineapple juice
 1 egg white*

Dissolve gelatin and salt in boiling water. Add pineapple juice. Place bowl of gelatin in larger bowl of ice water; stir until slightly thickened. Add egg white. With electric mixer at medium speed, beat until fluffy, thick and about doubled in volume. Lightly spoon into serving bowl or individual dessert dishes. Chill until firm, about 3 hours. Garnish with pineapple chunks and mint leaves, if desired.

*Use only clean egg with no cracks in shell.

— ■ —

CREAMY PEACH SALAD

Makes about 3½ cups or 6 to 7 servings

1 package (4-serving size) JELL-O® Brand Peach Flavor
   Gelatin
1 cup boiling water
⅓ cup cold water
½ cup plain yogurt
1¾ cups thawed COOL WHIP® Non-Dairy Whipped Topping
1 can (16 ounces) sliced peaches, drained and chopped
¼ cup chopped nuts

Dissolve gelatin in boiling water. Add cold water. Chill until slightly thickened. Blend yogurt into whipped topping; then blend in gelatin. Stir in peaches and nuts. Pour into 8×4-inch loaf pan. Chill until firm, about 3 hours. Unmold. Garnish with additional peach slices, if desired.

STRAWBERRIES AND CREAM

Makes about 4 cups or 8 servings

2 cups cold milk

1 package (6-serving size) JELL-O® Vanilla Flavor Instant
    Pudding and Pie Filling

1 teaspoon vanilla

2 cups thawed COOL WHIP® Non-Dairy Whipped Topping

2 packages (10 ounces each) BIRDS EYE® Quick Thaw
    Strawberries in a Lite Syrup, thawed and drained

Pour cold milk into bowl. Add pudding mix and vanilla. With electric mixer at low speed, beat until well blended, 1 to 2 minutes. Fold in whipped topping. Chill 20 minutes or until pudding mixture is thick. Layer pudding mixture and strawberries in individual dessert dishes. Chill.

MILK WHIP

Makes 3 cups or 6 servings

¾ cup boiling water

1 package (4-serving size) JELL-O® Brand Sugar Free
    Gelatin, any flavor

½ cup cold whole milk

Ice cubes

Pour boiling water into blender. Add gelatin. Cover and blend at low speed until gelatin is completely dissolved, about 30 seconds. Combine cold milk and ice cubes to make 1¼ cups. Add to gelatin and stir until ice is partially melted; then blend at high speed for 30 seconds. Spoon into individual dessert dishes or serving bowl. Sprinkle with cinnamon or nutmeg, if desired. Chill until set, about 30 minutes.

Banana Whip: Prepare Milk Whip as directed, adding 1 medium banana, sliced, with the milk.

CUCUMBER SOUR CREAM RELISH

Makes 3 cups or 9 relish servings

1 package (4-serving size) JELL-O® Brand Lime Flavor
    Sugar Free Gelatin
¼ teaspoon salt
¾ cup boiling water
1 tablespoon lemon juice
½ cup cold water
    Ice cubes
½ cup sour cream
1 cup chopped seeded peeled cucumber
1 tablespoon minced onion
1 tablespoon minced fresh dill or 1 teaspoon dried
    dillweed, crumbled

Completely dissolve gelatin and salt in boiling water. Add lemon juice. Combine cold water and ice cubes to make 1¼ cups. Add to gelatin, stirring until slightly thickened. Remove any unmelted ice. Blend in sour cream; fold in remaining ingredients. Pour into serving bowl or individual dishes. Chill until set, about 30 minutes. Garnish with cucumber slices and endive, if desired.

Fruited Fruit Juice Gelatin

Makes 5 cups or 10 servings

2 packages (4-serving size) or 1 package (8-serving size)
    JELL-O® Brand Orange Flavor Sugar Free Gelatin*
1½ cups boiling water
1 cup cold apple juice*
    Ice cubes
1½ cups diced apples*

Completely dissolve gelatin in boiling water. Combine cold fruit juice and ice cubes to make 2½ cups. Add to gelatin, stirring until slightly thickened. Remove any unmelted ice. Stir in apples. Pour into bowl or individual

CONTINUED

dessert glasses. Chill until set, about 4 hours. Garnish with celery leaves and additional fruit, if desired.

*Additional Flavor Combinations
Use strawberry flavor gelatin with canned pineapple juice, 1½ cups diced apples and ¼ cup chopped nuts.

Use raspberry flavor gelatin with cranberry juice cocktail, 1½ cups diced oranges, 2 tablespoons chopped nuts and ¼ cup chopped celery.

Use strawberry-banana flavor gelatin with orange juice and 1½ cups sliced bananas.

Use strawberry flavor gelatin with grape juice and 1½ cups seedless green grapes.

MOCHA-SPICE PARFAIT

Makes 3¼ cups or 6 servings

- 1 **package (4-serving size) JELL-O® Chocolate or Vanilla Flavor Sugar Free Pudding and Pie Filling**
- 2 **cups low-fat milk**
- 1 **tablespoon MAXWELL HOUSE® or YUBAN® Instant Coffee**
- ¼ **teaspoon cinnamon**
- 1½ **cups thawed COOL WHIP® Non-Dairy Whipped Topping**

Range Top: Combine pudding mix, milk and instant coffee in medium saucepan; blend well. Cook and stir over medium heat until mixture comes to a full boil. Pour into bowl; cover surface of pudding with plastic wrap. Chill. Mix cinnamon with whipped topping. Layer pudding and topping in individual parfait glasses or serving bowl. Chill.

Microwave:* Combine pudding mix, milk and instant coffee in 1½-quart microwave-safe bowl; blend well. Cook at HIGH 3 minutes. Stir well and cook 2 minutes longer; then stir again and cook 1 minute or until mixture comes to a boil. Stir; cover surface of pudding with plastic wrap. Chill. Mix cinnamon with whipped topping. Layer pudding and topping in individual parfait glasses or serving bowl. Chill.

*Ovens vary. Cooking time is approximate.

SPECIAL OCCASIONS

For an unforgettable celebration, dazzle your
guests with one of these glittering
temptations. These exceptional recipes require
a bit more effort, but make-ahead ease
lets the cook enjoy the party too!

Strawberry Bavarian Pie

STRAWBERRY BAVARIAN PIE

Makes one 9-inch pie

1 package (4-serving size) JELL-O® Brand Strawberry
    Flavor Gelatin
¼ cup sugar
1 cup boiling water
¼ cup cold water
1 pint strawberries, hulled and halved
1¾ cups thawed COOL WHIP® Non-Dairy Whipped Topping
1 baked 9-inch pie shell, cooled

Dissolve gelatin and sugar in boiling water. Add cold water. Chill until thickened. Arrange strawberries in bottom of pie shell. With electric mixer at medium speed, beat thickened gelatin until fluffy, thick and about doubled in volume. Blend in 1 cup of the whipped topping. Chill until mixture mounds. Spoon over berries in pie shell. Chill about 4 hours. Garnish with remaining whipped topping and additional berries, if desired.

CHERRIES JUBILEE SALAD

Makes about 5⅔ cups or 8 to 10 servings

1 can (20 ounces) pineapple chunks in juice
2 cans (6 ounces each) pineapple juice
2 packages (4-serving size) or 1 package (8-serving size)
    JELL-O® Brand Cherry Flavor Gelatin
½ cup red wine or water
½ teaspoon nutmeg
1 package (12 ounces) frozen dark sweet cherries,
    thawed
½ cup chopped pecans

Drain pineapple, reserving juice. Combine reserved juice and the 2 cans pineapple juice in small saucepan. Bring to a boil over high heat. Dissolve gelatin in juice. Add wine and nutmeg. Chill until slightly thickened. Fold in pineapple, cherries and pecans. Pour into 1½-quart mold. Chill until firm, about 6 hours. Unmold onto crisp salad greens, if desired.

— ■ —

FLUFFY GRASSHOPPER PIE

Makes one 9-inch pie

1 package (4-serving size) JELL-O® Brand Lime Flavor
    Gelatin
⅔ cup boiling water
½ cup cold water
    Ice cubes
2 tablespoons green creme de menthe liqueur*
2 tablespoons white creme de cacao liqueur*
3½ cups (8 ounces) COOL WHIP® Non-Dairy Whipped
    Topping, thawed
1 prepared 9-inch chocolate cookie crumb crust, cooled

Completely dissolve gelatin in boiling water. Combine cold water and ice cubes to make 1¼ cups. Add to gelatin, stirring until slightly thickened. Remove any unmelted ice. Fold liqueurs into whipped topping. Using wire whisk, blend whipped-topping mixture into gelatin; then whip until smooth. Chill until mixture mounds. Spoon into pie crust. Chill about 2 hours. Garnish with mint, if desired.

*Substitution: Use ½ teaspoon peppermint extract.

CUCUMBER PINWHEEL MOLD

Makes 6 cups or 12 servings

2 medium cucumbers

1½ teaspoons salt

1 package (4-serving size) JELL-O® Brand Lemon Flavor
   Gelatin

1 package (4-serving size) JELL-O® Brand Lime Flavor
   Gelatin

2 cups boiling water

½ cup cold water

2 tablespoons vinegar

1 tablespoon minced fresh dill or 1 teaspoon dried
   dillweed, crumbled

1 cup (½ pint) sour cream

Cut 20 thin slices from 1 of the cucumbers. Chop remaining cucumber (about 2 cups). Mix chopped cucumber with 1 teaspoon of the salt. Let stand 15 minutes; drain.

Dissolve both flavors of gelatin and remaining salt in boiling water. Add cold water and vinegar; chill until slightly thickened. Measure 1 cup of the gelatin mixture; pour ½ cup into 6-cup ring mold and chill until set but not firm. Arrange cucumber slices on gelatin in mold, pressing down lightly. Pour remaining measured gelatin over cucumber slices. Chill until set but not firm. Stir chopped cucumber, dill and sour cream into remaining gelatin; spoon into mold. Chill until firm, about 4 hours. Unmold.

— ■ —

ZUPPA INGLESE

Makes 6 servings

2 tablespoons slivered blanched almonds
1 package (4-serving size) JELL-O® Vanilla Flavor Pudding
   and Pie Filling
2¼ cups milk
¼ cup hot water
½ cup apricot or peach preserves
2 teaspoons rum extract
4 slices pound cake, cut into strips
1 tablespoon grated BAKER'S® GERMAN'S® Sweet
   Chocolate
Confectioners sugar

Toast almonds in shallow pan in preheated 350° oven for 3 to 5 minutes;
set aside. Combine pudding mix and milk in medium saucepan. Cook and
stir over medium heat until mixture comes to a full boil. Chill about 30
minutes. Blend water into preserves; add rum extract. Arrange cake strips
evenly around side of 1-quart serving bowl and spoon apricot mixture over
cake. Pour chilled pudding into cake-lined bowl. Chill thoroughly. Just
before serving, sprinkle pudding with almonds, chocolate and confectioners sugar.

CREAMY MELON LAYERED SALAD

Makes 3 cups or 6 servings

1 package (4-serving size) JELL-O® Brand Lemon or Lime
   Flavor Gelatin
1 cup boiling water
¾ cup cold water
1 teaspoon lemon juice
½ to 1 cup cantaloupe or honeydew melon balls or diced melon
   (about 1 small)
¼ cup sliced celery
¼ cup slivered almonds (optional)
1 package (3 ounces) cream cheese, softened
⅓ cup mayonnaise

CONTINUED

— ■ —

Dissolve gelatin in boiling water. Add cold water and lemon juice. Chill until slightly thickened. Measure 1¼ cups of the gelatin; fold in melon balls, celery and nuts. Pour into 4-cup ring mold or individual molds. Chill until set but not firm.

Blend cream cheese and mayonnaise until smooth. Gradually blend in remaining gelatin. Pour over clear gelatin in mold. Chill until firm, about 3 hours. Unmold. Garnish with additional melon balls and crisp greens, if desired.

Left to right: Peach Melba Parfait (see page 148), Topaz Parfait, Banana-Rum Parfait

— ◼ —

TOPAZ PARFAIT

Makes 4 to 6 servings

- 1 cup brewed MAXWELL HOUSE® or YUBAN® Coffee
- 1 package (4-serving size) JELL-O® Brand Lemon Flavor Gelatin
- ⅓ cup granulated sugar
- ½ cup cold water
- ¼ cup brandy or dark rum
- 2 tablespoons brown sugar
- 1 tablespoon brandy or dark rum
- 1¾ cups thawed COOL WHIP® Non-Dairy Whipped Topping

Bring coffee to a boil. Add gelatin and granulated sugar; stir until dissolved. Add cold water and the ¼ cup brandy. Pour into 8-inch square pan. Chill until firm, about 4 hours.

Cut gelatin into cubes or flake with fork. Fold brown sugar and the 1 tablespoon brandy into whipped topping. Layer gelatin cubes and topping in parfait glasses or top cubes in dessert glasses with topping.

BANANA-RUM PARFAIT

Makes 2¾ cups or 5 servings

- 1 package (4-serving size) JELL-O® Brand Lemon, Orange or Strawberry Flavor Gelatin
- 1 cup boiling water
- ¼ cup cold water
  Ice cubes
- 1 medium banana, sliced
- 1 cup (½ pint) vanilla ice cream
- 1 tablespoon light rum or ¼ teaspoon rum extract

Completely dissolve gelatin in boiling water. Measure ½ cup of the gelatin. Combine cold water and ice cubes to make ¾ cup. Add to measured gelatin, stirring until slightly thickened. Remove any unmelted ice. Stir in banana and spoon into individual parfait glasses. Blend ice cream and rum into remaining gelatin. Spoon over fruited gelatin in glasses. Chill until set, about 30 minutes. Garnish as desired.

— ◼ —

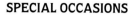

PEACH MELBA PARFAIT

Makes about 2½ cups or 5 servings

1 package (3 ounces) cream cheese, softened
1 tablespoon sugar
1 tablespoon milk
1 package (4-serving size) JELL-O® Brand Peach Flavor Gelatin
¾ cup boiling water
½ cup cold water
  Ice cubes
1 cup diced peeled peaches or 1 can (8¾ ounces) peaches, drained and diced
¼ cup raspberry jam or preserves

Combine cream cheese, sugar and milk in bowl. With electric mixer at medium speed, blend well; set aside. Completely dissolve gelatin in boiling water. Combine cold water and ice cubes to make 1¼ cups. Add to gelatin, stirring until slightly thickened. Remove any unmelted ice. Fold in peaches.

Spoon half of the fruited gelatin into parfait or wine glasses. Carefully spoon about 1 tablespoon of the cheese mixture over fruited gelatin in each glass; add scant tablespoon of the jam. Spoon remaining fruited gelatin over jam in glasses. Chill until set, about 2 hours. Garnish with whipped topping and peach slices, if desired.

STRAWBERRY LOAF

Makes about 6 cups or 12 servings

12 ladyfingers, split
1 pint strawberries, hulled
2 packages (4-serving size) or 1 package (8-serving size) JELL-O® Brand Strawberry Flavor Gelatin
2 cups boiling water
1 cup cold water
½ teaspoon almond extract
1¾ cups thawed COOL WHIP® Non-Dairy Whipped Topping

CONTINUED

Line sides of 9×5-inch loaf pan with ladyfingers; trim tops of ladyfingers, if necessary. Cut 1 cup of the strawberries into halves; slice remaining berries. Dissolve gelatin in boiling water. Add cold water. Measure ¾ cup of the gelatin. Chill until thickened. Spoon into pan and arrange strawberry halves, cut-side up, in rows on gelatin.

Add extract to remaining gelatin. Chill until slightly thickened. Fold in whipped topping and the sliced strawberries. Spoon over strawberry halves in pan. Chill until firm, about 4 hours. Unmold onto serving plate. Garnish with additional whipped topping, if desired.

CARROT-PINEAPPLE RELISH

Makes 3½ cups

2½ cups shredded carrots
1 can (8¼ ounces) crushed pineapple
1 cup sugar
1 cup water
⅓ cup vinegar
1 package (4-serving size) JELL-O® Brand Lemon Flavor
  Gelatin

Combine carrots, undrained pineapple, sugar, water and vinegar in medium saucepan. Bring to a boil over medium-high heat; reduce heat, then boil 10 minutes, stirring often. Remove from heat; add gelatin and stir until dissolved. Quickly ladle into hot sterilized jars or freezer containers.* Cover tightly. Cool and store in refrigerator or freezer. Relish can be refrigerated up to 2 weeks or frozen up to 6 months.

*Relish may be chilled in bowl; store, covered, in refrigerator for about 2 weeks.

CHOCOLATE ALMOND PIE

Makes one 9-inch pie

Quick Coconut Crust (recipe follows)
⅔ cup slivered blanched almonds
1 package (6-serving size) JELL-O® Chocolate Flavor
    Pudding and Pie Filling
3 cups milk
¼ teaspoon almond extract
1 cup thawed COOL WHIP® Non-Dairy Whipped Topping

Prepare Quick Coconut Crust; set aside. Toast almonds in shallow pan in preheated 350° oven for 3 to 5 minutes, stirring once. Chop ½ cup of the almonds; reserve remaining almonds for garnish.

Combine pie filling mix and milk in medium saucepan; blend well. Cook and stir over medium heat until mixture comes to a full boil. Cool 5 minutes, stirring twice. Stir in chopped nuts and extract. Pour into pie crust and cover surface of filling with plastic wrap. Chill about 4 hours. Remove plastic wrap. Garnish with whipped topping and reserved nuts.

Quick Coconut Crust: Combine ⅓ cup butter or margarine, melted, and 2⅔ cups BAKER'S® ANGEL FLAKE® Coconut in medium bowl. Evenly press into ungreased 9-inch pie pan. Bake in preheated 300° oven for 20 to 30 minutes, or until golden brown. Cool on wire rack.

Note: For ease in serving, dip pie pan just to rim in warm water for a few seconds; then cut and serve.

Top to bottom: French Cherry Pie (see page 152),
Chocolate Almond Pie, Praline Ice Cream Pudding Pie (see page 152) ▶

— ■ —

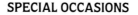

PRALINE ICE CREAM PUDDING PIE

Makes one 9-inch pie

2 tablespoons light brown sugar
2 tablespoons butter or margarine
⅓ cup chopped nuts
1 lightly baked 9-inch pie shell*
1½ cups cold milk
1 cup (½ pint) vanilla ice cream, softened
1 package (6-serving size) JELL-O® Butter Pecan Flavor
    Instant Pudding and Pie Filling

Combine brown sugar, butter and nuts in small saucepan. Heat over medium heat until butter is melted. Pour into pie shell. Bake in preheated 450° oven for 5 minutes or until bubbly. Cool on wire rack.

Combine milk and ice cream in medium bowl until thoroughly blended. Add pie filling mix. With electric mixer at low speed, beat until blended, about 1 minute. Pour immediately over nut mixture in pie shell. Chill until set, about 3 hours. Garnish with whipped topping and pecan halves or chopped nuts, if desired.

*Decrease recommended baking time by 5 minutes.

FRENCH CHERRY PIE

Makes one 8-inch pie

1 cup cold milk
1 cup (½ pint) sour cream
¼ teaspoon almond extract
1 package (4-serving size) JELL-O® Vanilla or French
    Vanilla Flavor Instant Pudding and Pie Filling
1 prepared 8-inch graham cracker crumb crust or baked
    pie shell, cooled
1 can (21 ounces) cherry pie filling

Combine cold milk, sour cream and almond extract in bowl. Add pie filling mix. With electric mixer at low speed, beat until blended, about 1 minute. Pour immediately into pie crust. Chill about 2 hours. Spoon cherry pie filling over pie.

FRUIT BOWL

Makes 6 cups or 12 servings

2 packages (4-serving size) or 1 package (8-serving size)
  JELL-O® Brand Lemon Flavor Gelatin
1½ cups boiling water
1 cup ginger ale
  Ice cubes
1 small apple, cored and sliced
1 cup melon balls
½ cup halved seedless grapes
1 small pear, peeled, cored and sliced
1 cup orange sections

Completely dissolve gelatin in boiling water. Combine ginger ale and ice cubes to make 2½ cups. Add to gelatin, stirring until slightly thickened. Remove any unmelted ice. Chill until thickened, about 10 minutes. Arrange apple slices in 6-cup serving bowl. Add enough gelatin to just cover apples. Repeat layering with remaining fruit and gelatin. Chill until set, about 1 hour. Garnish with additional fruit, if desired.

CREME BRULÉE

Makes 4½ cups or 8 to 10 servings

1 package (6-serving size) JELL-O® Vanilla Flavor Pudding
  and Pie Filling
1 quart light cream or half and half
2 eggs, slightly beaten
1 teaspoon vanilla
¼ cup packed brown sugar, sieved

Combine pudding mix and cream in medium saucepan; blend well. Cook and stir over medium heat until mixture comes to a full boil. Remove from heat. Stir small amount of hot mixture into eggs, mixing well. Return egg mixture to remaining hot mixture, stirring constantly. Cook over low heat for 1 minute, stirring constantly. Add vanilla and pour into shallow 1½-quart baking dish. Chill at least 3 hours. Evenly sprinkle brown sugar over top of pudding. Broil until sugar melts, about 1½ minutes. Serve warm or chill. Serve over fruit or cake, if desired.

RAINBOW CAKE

Makes 12 servings

1 package (4-serving size) JELL-O® Brand Raspberry
   Flavor Gelatin
1 package (4-serving size) JELL-O® Brand Lemon Flavor
   Gelatin
1 package (4-serving size) JELL-O® Brand Lime Flavor
   Gelatin
3 cups boiling water
2¼ cups cold water
1¾ cups thawed COOL WHIP® Non-Dairy Whipped Topping
½ cup BAKER'S® ANGEL FLAKE® Coconut

Dissolve gelatin flavors separately, using 1 cup of the boiling water for
each flavor. Add ¾ cup of the cold water to each flavor. Place bowl of
raspberry flavor gelatin in larger bowl of ice and water. Stir until slightly
thickened; then with electric mixer at medium speed, beat until fluffy,
thick and about doubled in volume. Pour into 9- or 10-inch springform pan
or 10-inch tube pan. Chill until set but not firm.

Repeat chilling and beating procedure with lemon flavor gelatin. Pour over
raspberry flavor gelatin in pan. Chill until set but not firm. Repeat chilling
and beating procedure with lime flavor gelatin. Pour over lemon flavor
gelatin in pan. Chill until firm. Unmold onto serving plate. Spread whipped
topping over top of gelatin; sprinkle with coconut. Cut into wedges.

PINA COLADA PIE

Makes one 9-inch pie

1 package (4-serving size) JELL-O® Lemon or Vanilla
   Flavor Instant Pudding and Pie Filling
1½ cups sour cream
3 tablespoons rum*
2 tablespoons sugar
2 tablespoons milk*
1 teaspoon grated lime rind
1 can (8¼ ounces) crushed pineapple, drained

CONTINUED

— ∎ —

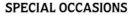
1 cup BAKER'S® ANGEL FLAKE® Coconut, plain or
   toasted
1 baked 9-inch pie shell or prepared graham cracker crumb
   crust, cooled

Combine pie filling mix, sour cream, rum, sugar, milk and rind in medium bowl. With electric mixer at low speed, beat until blended and smooth, about 1 minute. Fold in pineapple and coconut. Spoon into pie shell. Chill about 3 hours. Garnish with whipped topping, fruit and mint leaves, if desired.

*Substitution: Use ½ teaspoon rum extract, increasing milk to ¼ cup.

CHIFFON PARTY DESSERT

Makes 5 cups or 10 servings

2 packages (4-serving size) or 1 package (8-serving size)
JELL-O® Brand Black Raspberry, Orange or Black
Cherry Flavor Gelatin

2 cups boiling water

1 quart vanilla ice cream

12 ladyfingers, split

CONTINUED

Completely dissolve gelatin in boiling water. Add ice cream by spoonfuls, stirring until completely melted. Chill until thickened.

Meanwhile, trim off about 1 inch of the ladyfingers and place cut ends down around side of 8-inch springform pan. Spoon gelatin mixture into pan. Chill until firm, about 3 hours. Remove side of pan. Garnish with whipped topping, fresh fruit and mint leaves, if desired.

FRESH FRUIT MOUSSE

Makes 6 cups or 12 servings

1 cup boiling water
1 package (4-serving size) JELL-O® Brand Lemon or
    Strawberry Flavor Gelatin*
¾ cup sugar
1 pint strawberries, hulled*
2 egg whites**
1¾ cups thawed COOL WHIP® Non-Dairy Whipped Topping

Pour boiling water into blender. Add gelatin and ½ cup of the sugar. Cover and blend at low speed until completely dissolved, about 30 seconds. Blend in strawberries, a few at a time, at high speed until pureed. Chill until slightly thickened, about 2 hours.

With electric mixer at medium speed, beat egg whites until foamy. Gradually add remaining sugar, beating thoroughly after each addition. Continue beating at high speed until mixture forms stiff shiny peaks. Fold in whipped topping; then fold in thickened fruit mixture. Spoon into dessert glasses. Garnish with additional whipped topping, if desired.

*Additional Flavor Combinations
Use peach flavor gelatin with 2 medium peeled and quartered peaches.

Use lemon flavor gelatin with 3 peeled and quartered plums.

Use lime flavor gelatin with 2 medium peeled, cored and quartered pears.

**Use only clean eggs with no cracks in shells.

GLAZED FRUIT PIE

Makes one 9-inch pie

1½ cups cold milk or half and half

1 package (4-serving size) JELL-O® Vanilla Flavor Instant Pudding and Pie Filling

1 baked 9-inch pie shell or prepared graham cracker crumb crust, cooled

1 package (4-serving size) JELL-O® Brand Peach or Orange Flavor Gelatin, or any red flavor

1 cup boiling water

½ cup cold water

2 cups (about) fresh or drained canned fruit*

Pour cold milk into bowl. Add pie filling mix. With electric mixer at low speed, beat 1 minute. Pour into pie shell. Chill 1 hour.

Dissolve gelatin in boiling water. Add cold water. Chill until thickened. Pour about ½ cup of the gelatin over pie filling in pie shell. Arrange fruit on gelatin and spoon remaining gelatin over fruit. Chill about 2 hours.

*Do not use fresh pineapple, kiwifruit, mango, papaya or figs.

PINEAPPLE RASPBERRY TORTE

Makes 12 servings

1 package (4-serving size) JELL-O® Brand Raspberry Flavor Gelatin

1¼ cups boiling water

1 can (20 ounces) crushed pineapple

2 baked 9-inch white cake layers, cooled

1¾ cups thawed COOL WHIP® Non-Dairy Whipped Topping

Dissolve gelatin in boiling water. Stir in undrained pineapple and chill until very thick. Spread half of the gelatin mixture on top of each cake layer and chill until firm, about 3 hours. Spread half of the whipped topping over the gelatin on 1 layer. Top with remaining layer, gelatin-side up, and remaining whipped topping. Chill.

Glazed Fruit Pie

—■—

PUDDING CHARLOTTE

Makes 6 servings

1 package (4-serving size) JELL-O® Milk Chocolate,
　　Chocolate, Coconut Cream, Vanilla or French Vanilla
　　Flavor Pudding and Pie Filling
2 cups milk
9 ladyfingers, split
¼ cup strawberry or apricot jam
1¾ cups thawed COOL WHIP® Non-Dairy Whipped Topping
1 teaspoon lemon rind*

Combine pudding mix and milk in medium saucepan; blend well. Cook and stir over medium heat until mixture comes to a full boil. Remove from heat and place plastic wrap directly on surface of hot pudding. Chill about 2 hours.

Spread ladyfingers with jam and press together; cut each in half crosswise. Blend 1 cup of the whipped topping and the lemon rind into chilled pudding. Spoon about half the pudding mixture into shallow 1-quart serving bowl. Line sides with filled ladyfinger halves; then spoon in remaining pudding mixture. Chill. Garnish with remaining whipped topping and toasted almond halves, toasted coconut or maraschino cherries, if desired.

*Omit lemon rind with chocolate, milk chocolate or coconut cream flavor pudding and pie filling.

LAYERED CHERRY CHOCOLATE PARFAIT

Makes about 6 cups or 12 servings

1 can (16 ounces) pitted dark sweet cherries
2 packages (4-serving size) or 1 package (8-serving size)
　　JELL-O® Brand Cherry Flavor Gelatin
1½ cups cold water
2 cups (1 pint) chocolate ice cream, softened
2 cups thawed COOL WHIP® Non-Dairy Whipped Topping

Drain cherries, reserving syrup. Chop cherries; set aside. Add water to syrup to make 2 cups; place in medium saucepan. Bring to a boil over high

CONTINUED

——

heat. Dissolve gelatin in boiling liquid. Measure 1½ cups of the gelatin; add cold water. Chill until thickened.

Meanwhile, add ice cream to remaining gelatin, stirring until smooth. Pour into 8-cup serving bowl. Chill until set but not firm. Spoon whipped topping over ice cream layer in bowl.

Fold cherries into thickened gelatin. Carefully spoon over whipped topping in bowl. Chill until set, about 3 hours. Garnish with additional whipped topping and chocolate curls, if desired.

PEAR-PINEAPPLE MOLD

Makes about 6 cups or 12 servings

½ cup blanched almonds
1 can (8¼ ounces) crushed pineapple in juice
2 packages (4-serving size) or 1 package (8-serving size)
   JELL-O® Brand Lime Flavor Gelatin
2 cups boiling water
1 medium pear
   Halved maraschino cherries
⅔ cup sour cream
⅓ cup mayonnaise
¼ cup well-drained chopped maraschino cherries

Toast almonds in shallow pan in preheated 350° oven for 3 to 5 minutes, stirring once. Chop nuts; set aside. Drain pineapple, reserving juice. Add water to juice to make 1 cup. Dissolve gelatin in boiling water. Add measured liquid and chill until slightly thickened. Measure 1½ cups of the gelatin and pour into 6-cup mold. Peel and core pear; cut half of the pear into thin slices and dice the other half. Arrange pear slices and halved cherries on top of clear gelatin in mold. Chill until set but not firm. Combine sour cream and mayonnaise; blend in remaining gelatin. Chill until thickened. Stir in diced pear, the pineapple, nuts and chopped cherries. Spoon over gelatin in mold. Chill until firm, about 4 hours. Unmold.

CROWD PLEASERS

THE JELL-O

PAGES

When the gang gathers for food
and fun, you'll turn to these mouth-watering
specialties again and again. All the
recipes are crowd-size, and many are just
right for take-along convenience.

Cherry-Topped Icebox Cake

CHERRY-TOPPED ICEBOX CAKE

Makes 12 servings

20 whole graham crackers

2 cups cold milk

1 package (6-serving size) JELL-O® Vanilla or Chocolate
   Flavor Instant Pudding and Pie Filling

1¾ cups thawed COOL WHIP® Non-Dairy Whipped Topping

2 cans (21 ounces each) cherry pie filling

Line 13×9-inch pan with some of the graham crackers, breaking crackers, if necessary. Pour cold milk into bowl. Add pudding mix. With electric mixer at low speed, beat until well blended, 1 to 2 minutes. Let stand 5 minutes; then blend in whipped topping. Spread half of the pudding mixture over crackers. Add another layer of crackers. Top with remaining pudding mixture and remaining crackers. Spread cherry pie filling over crackers. Chill about 3 hours.

Chocolate-Frosted Icebox Cake: Prepare Cherry-Topped Icebox Cake as directed, substituting ¾ cup ready-to-spread chocolate fudge frosting for the cherry pie filling. Carefully spread frosting over top layer of graham crackers.

FROZEN FRUIT SALAD

Makes 6 cups or 12 servings

1 package (4-serving size) JELL-O® Brand Strawberry
   Flavor Gelatin

1 cup boiling water

1 can (6 fluid ounces) frozen concentrated lemonade

3 cups thawed COOL WHIP® Non-Dairy Whipped Topping

1 can (16 ounces) sliced peaches, drained and chopped

1 can (8½ ounces) pear halves, drained and chopped

Completely dissolve gelatin in boiling water. Add lemonade and stir until melted. Chill until slightly thickened. Blend in whipped topping and fold in fruit. Pour into 9×5-inch loaf pan. Freeze until firm, about 4 hours. Remove from freezer about 30 minutes before serving. Unmold and slice.

CONTINENTAL CHEESE MOLD

Makes 4 cups or 12 servings

- 1 package (4-serving size) JELL-O® Brand Lemon Flavor Gelatin
- ¾ cup boiling water
- 2 cups (16 ounces) cottage cheese
- ½ cup sour cream
- ¼ pound Roquefort or bleu cheese, softened*
- 2 teaspoons seasoned salt
- ¾ teaspoon Worcestershire sauce
- ½ teaspoon lemon juice
- 2 tablespoons finely cut chives or parsley

CONTINUED

Dissolve gelatin in boiling water. Combine cottage cheese, sour cream, Roquefort cheese, salt, Worcestershire sauce and lemon juice in large bowl; with electric mixer at low speed, beat until smooth. Gradually blend in gelatin. Stir in chives and pour into 4-cup mold. Chill until firm, about 3 hours. Unmold. Serve as an appetizer with assorted crackers and fresh vegetables, if desired.

*Cheese may be crumbled and folded in with chives.

BLEU CHEESE SPREAD

Makes about 6 cups or 12 servings

2 packages (4-serving size) or 1 package (8-serving size) JELL-O® Brand Lime Flavor Gelatin
1½ cups boiling water
½ cup cold water
   Ice cubes
1 package (8 ounces) cream cheese, softened
¼ cup crumbled bleu cheese
1½ cups mayonnaise
1 cup (½ pint) sour cream
1 tablespoon vinegar
¾ teaspoon salt
¾ cup finely chopped scallions
½ cup finely chopped parsley

Completely dissolve gelatin in boiling water. Combine cold water and ice cubes to make 1 cup. Add to gelatin, stirring until ice melts. Remove any unmelted ice. With electric mixer at medium speed, beat cream cheese and bleu cheese in large bowl until smooth. Blend in mayonnaise, sour cream, vinegar and salt. Gradually blend in gelatin. Chill until thickened. Fold in scallions and parsley. Pour into 8-cup bowl. Chill until set, about 3 hours. Garnish with carrot curls, radish and parsley, if desired. Serve with assorted crackers.

LAYERED PEACH MELBA DESSERT

Makes 15 servings

1½ cups graham cracker crumbs

¼ cup sugar

⅓ cup butter or margarine, melted

3½ cups (8 ounces) COOL WHIP® Non-Dairy Whipped
  Topping, thawed

1 cup (½ pint) sour cream

1½ cups plus 2 tablespoons cold milk

1 package (8 ounces) cream cheese, softened

1 package (6-serving size) JELL-O® Vanilla Flavor Instant
  Pudding and Pie Filling

1 can (16 ounces) sliced peaches, drained and diced

½ cup raspberry preserves

Combine crumbs, sugar and butter; mix well. Press firmly onto bottom of 13×9-inch pan. Bake in preheated 375° oven for about 8 minutes. Cool on wire rack.

Combine whipped topping, sour cream and 2 tablespoons of the milk in large bowl. With electric mixer at low speed, blend well. Measure 1 cup of the sour cream mixture; set aside. Add cream cheese to remaining sour cream mixture; beat until smooth. Add remaining milk and the pie filling mix. Blend at low speed for about 1 minute, scraping sides of bowl frequently. Spread evenly on crust. Evenly spread peaches over pie filling mixture. Spread reserved sour cream mixture over peaches. (If sour cream mixture thickens, thin with a little milk.) Chill about 4 hours. Just before serving, garnish with additional peach slices, if desired, and the raspberry preserves.

Layered Cherry Dessert: Prepare Layered Peach Melba Dessert as directed, omitting peaches and raspberry preserves. Just before serving, spoon 1 can (21 ounces) cherry pie filling over top of dessert.

WINTER FRUIT BOWL

Makes about 6½ cups or 12 servings

2 packages (4-serving size) or 1 package (8-serving size)
    JELL-O® Brand Lemon Flavor Gelatin

1½ cups boiling water

1 can (12 fluid ounces) lemon-lime carbonated beverage,
    chilled

Ice cubes

3 cups diced or sliced fresh fruits* (bananas, oranges,
    apples, pears, grapes)

Dissolve gelatin in boiling water. Combine beverage and ice cubes to make 2½ cups. Add to gelatin, stirring until slightly thickened. Remove any unmelted ice. Chill until thickened, about 10 minutes. Fold in fruits. Pour into 8-cup serving bowl. Chill until set, about 3 hours. Garnish with whipped topping and orange sections, if desired.

*Do not use fresh pineapple, kiwifruit, mango, papaya or figs.

—■—

FRUIT AND PUDDING TARTS

Makes 12 servings

1 package (4-serving size) JELL-O® Banana Cream,
  Coconut Cream, Vanilla or French Vanilla Flavor
  Pudding and Pie Filling
2 teaspoons lemon juice
1 egg, slightly beaten
2 cups milk
1 tablespoon butter or margarine
3½ cups diced fresh or drained frozen or canned fruit
12 baked 3-inch tart shells, cooled

Combine pudding mix, lemon juice and egg in medium saucepan; gradually stir in milk. Cook and stir over medium heat until mixture comes to a full boil. Remove from heat and stir in butter. Cool 5 minutes, stirring twice. Place fruit in tart shells, reserving some of the fruit for garnish, if desired. Spoon pudding over fruit in tart shells. Chill about 1 hour. Garnish with reserved fruit and whipped topping, if desired.

STRAWBERRY PISTACHIO TRIFLE

Makes 6 cups or 12 servings

4 slices pound cake, ½ inch thick
1 pint strawberries, hulled
2 tablespoons sugar
2 cups cold milk
2 packages (4-serving size) JELL-O® Pistachio Flavor
  Instant Pudding and Pie Filling
1¾ cups thawed COOL WHIP® Non-Dairy Whipped Topping

Cut each pound cake slice into 9 cubes. Place in 2-quart bowl or individual dessert dishes. Set aside 6 to 8 berries for garnish. Crush remaining berries and sprinkle with sugar. Spoon over cake cubes in bowl.

Pour cold milk into bowl. Add pudding mix. With electric mixer at low speed, beat until well blended, 1 to 2 minutes. Fold in whipped topping. Spoon over berries in bowl. Chill. Garnish with reserved strawberries, sliced, and additional whipped topping, if desired.

LEMON SNOW PUDDING

Makes 5¾ cups or 9 servings

1 package (4-serving size) JELL-O® Lemon Flavor Pudding
   and Pie Filling
1 package (4-serving size) JELL-O® Brand Lemon Flavor
   Gelatin
¾ cup sugar
2¾ cups water
2 eggs, separated

Combine pudding mix, gelatin, ½ cup of the sugar and ¼ cup of the water in medium saucepan. Blend in egg yolks and remaining water. Cook and stir over medium heat until mixture comes to a full boil. Remove from heat.

With electric mixer at medium speed, beat egg whites until foamy. Gradually add remaining sugar and continue beating at high speed until mixture forms stiff shiny peaks. Quickly fold into hot pudding, blending well. Pour into 8- or 9-inch square pan. Chill about 3 hours. Cut into squares. Serve with fresh fruit, if desired.

BANANA AND SOUR CREAM MOLD

Makes about 5 cups or 10 servings

  2 packages (4-serving size) JELL-O® Brand Lime or Lemon
    Flavor Gelatin
  2 cups boiling water
1¼ cups cold water
  1 small banana, sliced
½ cup sour cream
¼ cup diced celery
¼ cup chopped walnuts or pecans

CONTINUED

Dissolve 1 package of the gelatin in 1 cup of the boiling water. Add ¾ cup of the cold water and chill until thickened. Stir in banana and spoon into 6-cup ring mold. Chill until set but not firm, about 15 minutes.

Meanwhile, dissolve remaining gelatin in remaining boiling water. Add remaining cold water and chill until slightly thickened. Blend in sour cream. Stir in celery and nuts. Spoon over fruited gelatin in mold. Chill until firm, about 4 hours. Unmold. Garnish with lettuce and walnut halves, if desired.

CHURCH SUPPER SPECIAL DESSERT

Makes 20 servings

1¼ cups graham cracker crumbs
 ¼ cup sugar
 ¼ cup butter or margarine, melted
 2 packages (4-serving size) or 1 package (8-serving size)
    JELL-O® Brand Gelatin, any red flavor
 2 cups boiling water
1½ cups cold water
 1 pound marshmallows (about 4 cups)
 1 cup milk
 3 medium bananas, sliced
1¾ cups thawed COOL WHIP® Non-Dairy Whipped Topping

Combine crumbs, sugar and butter; mix well. Press firmly on bottom of 13×9-inch pan. Chill for at least 15 minutes. Dissolve gelatin in boiling water. Add cold water. Chill until slightly thickened.

Combine marshmallows and milk in medium saucepan. Heat over low heat until marshmallows are melted, stirring constantly. Cool completely.

Arrange banana slices in single layer on crumb crust in pan. Blend whipped topping into cooled marshmallow mixture; swirl slightly into thickened gelatin for marbled effect. Pour over bananas in pan. Chill until firm, about 3 hours. Cut into squares. Garnish with additional whipped topping, if desired.

BANANA-CHEESE SQUARES

Makes 12 servings

½ cup blanched almonds

1½ cups all-purpose flour

½ cup packed light brown sugar

½ cup butter or margarine, melted

1 package (8 ounces) cream cheese, softened

¼ cup milk

3½ cups (8 ounces) COOL WHIP® Non-Dairy Whipped
   Topping, thawed

2 packages (4-serving size) or 1 package (8-serving size)
   JELL-O® Brand Orange Flavor Gelatin

2 cups boiling water

1½ cups cold water

2 cups sliced bananas

1 cup orange sections

Toast almonds in shallow pan in preheated 350° oven for 3 to 5 minutes, stirring once. Chop almonds; set aside.

Combine flour, ¼ cup of the brown sugar and the butter in medium bowl. Mix well and evenly press into bottom of 13×9-inch pan. Bake in preheated 375° oven for about 20 minutes. Cool on wire rack.

Combine cream cheese and remaining brown sugar in large bowl. With electric mixer at medium speed, beat until blended. Gradually add milk and beat until smooth and creamy. Fold in whipped topping and spread evenly over pastry. Chill.

Dissolve gelatin in boiling water. Add cold water. Chill until slightly thickened. Fold in fruits and nuts. Spoon over cheese layer in pan. Chill until firm, about 4 hours. Cut into squares.

BUFFET LEMON CHEESECAKE

Makes 9 to 12 servings

1¼ cups graham cracker crumbs

3 tablespoons sugar

⅓ cup butter or margarine, melted

2 packages (8 ounces each) cream cheese, softened

4 cups cold milk

2 packages (4-serving size) JELL-O® Lemon Flavor Instant
   Pudding and Pie Filling

Combine crumbs, sugar and butter; mix well. Press firmly on bottom and side of 9- or 10-inch springform pan. Bake in preheated 350° oven for about 8 minutes, or until lightly browned. Cool on wire rack.

Place cream cheese in large bowl. With electric mixer at medium speed, beat until smooth. Gradually add 1 cup of the milk, blending until mixture is very smooth. Add remaining milk and the pudding mix. Beat at low speed just until well blended, about 1 minute. Pour carefully into crumb-lined pan. Chill until firm, about 3 hours. Garnish with lemon slice and mint, if desired.

CREAM CHEESE PUDDING DESSERT

Makes 15 servings

1½ cups graham cracker crumbs
½ cup sugar
⅓ cup butter or margarine, melted
1 package (8 ounces) cream cheese, softened
2½ cups plus 2 tablespoons milk
3½ cups (8 ounces) COOL WHIP® Non-Dairy Whipped
    Topping, thawed
1 package (6-serving size) JELL-O® Instant Pudding and
    Pie Filling, any flavor

CONTINUED

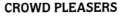
Combine crumbs, ¼ cup of the sugar and the butter; mix well. Press firmly into bottom of 13×9-inch pan. Chill 15 minutes.

Combine cream cheese, remaining sugar and 2 tablespoons of the milk in medium bowl. With electric mixer at medium speed, beat until smooth. Fold in 1¾ cups of the whipped topping. Spread over crust.

Pour remaining milk into bowl. Add pudding mix. With electric mixer at low speed, beat until well blended, 1 to 2 minutes. Pour over cream cheese layer in pan. Chill several hours. Just before serving, spread remaining whipped topping over pudding. Garnish with chocolate curls, if desired.

LAYERED BANANA PINEAPPLE DESSERT

Makes 15 servings

1½ cups graham cracker crumbs
¼ cup sugar
⅓ cup butter or margarine, melted
2 medium bananas, sliced
1 package (8 ounces) cream cheese, softened
2½ cups cold milk
1 package (6-serving size) JELL-O® Vanilla Flavor Instant Pudding and Pie Filling
1 can (20 ounces) crushed pineapple, drained
3½ cups (8 ounces) COOL WHIP® Non-Dairy Whipped Topping, thawed

Combine crumbs, sugar and butter; mix well. Press firmly on bottom of 13×9-inch pan. Bake in preheated 375° oven for about 8 minutes. Cool on wire rack.

Arrange sliced bananas on crust. With electric mixer at low speed, beat cream cheese until smooth. Gradually add ½ cup of the cold milk; blend until smooth. Add remaining milk and the pudding mix. Beat at low speed until well blended, about 2 minutes. Spread evenly over bananas in pan. Evenly spoon pineapple over pudding mixture. Spread whipped topping over pineapple. Chill about 3 hours.

PINEAPPLE CREAM CHEESE LOAF

Makes about 6½ cups or 12 servings

1 can (20 ounces) crushed pineapple in juice
2 packages (4-serving size) or 1 package (8-serving size)
    JELL-O® Brand Lime Flavor Gelatin
½ teaspoon salt (optional)
2 cups boiling water
2 tablespoons lemon juice
1 package (8 ounces) cream cheese, softened
¼ teaspoon ginger

Drain pineapple, reserving juice. Add cold water to juice to make 1½ cups. Dissolve gelatin and salt in boiling water. Add measured liquid and lemon juice. Measure 2½ cups of the gelatin; pour into 9×5-inch loaf pan or 6-cup mold. Chill until set but not firm.

Meanwhile, with electric mixer at medium speed, beat cream cheese and ginger until soft and creamy; very slowly blend in remaining gelatin. Stir in pineapple. Chill until slightly thickened. Spoon over clear gelatin in pan. Chill until firm, about 4 hours. Unmold. Serve as dessert or salad.

CROWN JEWEL DESSERT

Makes 8 cups or 16 servings

1 package (4-serving size) JELL-O® Brand Cherry Flavor
    Gelatin
1 package (4-serving size) JELL-O® Brand Lemon Flavor
    Gelatin
1 package (4-serving size) JELL-O® Brand Orange Flavor
    Gelatin
4 cups boiling water
1½ cups cold water
1 package (4-serving size) JELL-O® Brand Orange-
    Pineapple Flavor Gelatin
¼ cup sugar
½ cup cold canned pineapple juice
1¾ cups thawed COOL WHIP® Non-Dairy Whipped Topping

CONTINUED

Dissolve cherry, lemon and orange flavor gelatins separately, using 1 cup of the boiling water for each flavor. Add ½ cup of the cold water to each flavor. Pour each flavor into its own 8-inch square pan. Chill until firm, about 4 hours. Cut into ½-inch cubes.

Dissolve orange-pineapple flavor gelatin and sugar in remaining 1 cup boiling water. Add pineapple juice. Chill until slightly thickened. Blend whipped topping into orange-pineapple flavor gelatin. Fold in gelatin cubes. Pour into 9-inch tube pan or 8-cup mold. Chill overnight or until firm. Unmold. Garnish with whipped topping, if desired.

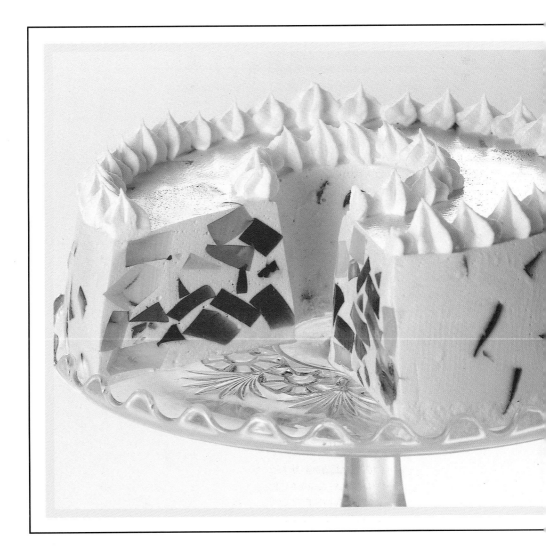

MOLDED CHEF'S SALAD

Makes about 6 cups or 10 to 12 servings

  2 packages (4-serving size) or 1 package (8-serving size)
      JELL-O® Brand Lemon Flavor Gelatin
1½ teaspoons salt
  2 cups boiling water
1½ cups cold water
  1 tablespoon vinegar
  ½ teaspoon Worcestershire sauce
  ⅛ teaspoon black pepper
  1 cup finely shredded lettuce
  ½ cup thin tomato wedges
  ½ cup finely shredded chicory or endive
  ¼ cup thinly sliced scallions
  ¼ cup thinly sliced radishes
  2 tablespoons thin strips green pepper
  1 tablespoon French dressing
  ½ cup slivered ham, tongue or veal
  ½ cup slivered Swiss cheese

CONTINUED

Dissolve gelatin and salt in boiling water. Add cold water, vinegar, Worcestershire sauce and pepper. Chill until slightly thickened.

Meanwhile, combine vegetables and dressing; let stand about 20 minutes to marinate. Fold vegetables, ham and cheese into gelatin. Pour into 6-cup ring mold or individual molds. Chill until firm, about 4 hours. Unmold. Serve with crisp salad greens and mayonnaise, if desired.

STRAWBERRY-PEACH UPSIDE DOWN CAKE

Makes one 13×9-inch cake

- 1 can (29 ounces) sliced peaches, drained, or 2 cups sliced peeled fresh peaches
- 1 package (4-serving size) JELL-O® Brand Strawberry Flavor Gelatin
- 1 package (4-serving size) JELL-O® Brand Peach Flavor Gelatin
- 1 teaspoon cinnamon (optional)
- ⅓ cup butter or margarine
- 1 package (2-layer size) yellow cake mix or pudding-included cake mix
  Ingredients for cake mix (see package)

Arrange peaches in buttered 13×9-inch pan. Combine strawberry and peach flavor gelatins and cinnamon in small bowl. Sprinkle about ¾ of the mixture evenly over peaches; dot with butter.

Prepare cake mix according to package directions. Pour ¾ of the batter into pan. Stir remaining gelatin mixture into remaining cake batter; blend well and pour over batter in pan. Swirl spatula through batter to marble. Bake in preheated 350° oven for 45 minutes, or until cake tester inserted in center of cake comes out clean and cake begins to pull away from sides of pan. Cool in pan on wire rack 5 minutes. Invert onto serving platter and cool. Garnish with whipped topping, if desired.

STRAWBERRY SQUARES

Makes 8 cups or 15 servings

1½ cups all-purpose flour

½ cup finely chopped pecans

½ cup butter or margarine, melted

2 packages (4-serving size) or 1 package (8-serving size)
JELL-O® Brand Strawberry Flavor Gelatin

2 packages (4-serving size) JELL-O® Vanilla Flavor
Pudding and Pie Filling

2½ cups water

3 pints strawberries, hulled and sliced

Combine flour, pecans and butter; mix well. Press evenly on bottom of 13×9-inch pan. Bake in preheated 375° oven for about 20 minutes. Cool on wire rack.

Combine gelatin, pie filling mix and water in medium saucepan; blend well. Cook and stir over medium heat until mixture comes to a boil. Remove from heat and stir in strawberries. Let stand about 5 minutes. Pour over cooled crust. Chill until set, about 5 hours. Garnish, if desired.

LAYERED COCONUT PECAN RECTANGLES

Makes 12 servings

1½ cups all-purpose flour

1 cup chopped pecans

½ cup butter or margarine, melted

2⅔ cups (about) BAKER'S® ANGEL FLAKE® Coconut

1 package (8 ounces) cream cheese, softened

3 cups cold milk

1 package (6-serving size) JELL-O® Vanilla Flavor Instant
Pudding and Pie Filling

3½ cups (8 ounces) COOL WHIP® Non-Dairy Whipped
Topping, thawed

Combine flour, ½ cup of the pecans and the butter; mix until flour is moistened. Press evenly on bottom of 13×9-inch pan. Bake in preheated 350° oven for about 15 minutes. Cool thoroughly on wire rack. Toast

CONTINUED

remaining pecans and ⅔ cup of the coconut on baking sheet in preheated 325° oven until lightly browned, about 5 minutes, stirring once. Set aside.

With electric mixer at low speed, beat cream cheese until very soft. Gradually add ½ cup of the cold milk; blend until smooth. Add remaining milk and the pudding mix. Beat at low speed until well blended, about 2 minutes. Stir in remaining coconut and immediately pour over baked crust. Evenly spread whipped topping over pudding. Sprinkle with toasted coconut and nuts. Chill about 2 hours. Cut into rectangles.

Note: Recipe may be doubled, using two 13×9-inch pans.

MOLDED STRAWBERRIES ROMANOFF

Makes 6 cups or 12 servings

1 **pint strawberries, hulled**
2 **tablespoons sugar**
2 **packages (4-serving size) or 1 package (8-serving size)**
   JELL-O® Brand Strawberry Flavor Gelatin
2 **cups boiling water**
2 **tablespoons brandy***
1 **tablespoon orange liqueur***
1¾ **cups thawed COOL WHIP® Non-Dairy Whipped Topping**

Slice strawberries, reserving a few whole berries for garnish, if desired. Sprinkle sliced berries with sugar; let stand 15 minutes. Drain, reserving liquid. Add water to liquid to make 1 cup. Dissolve gelatin in boiling water. Measure ¾ cup of the gelatin and add brandy, orange liqueur and ½ cup of the measured liquid. Chill until slightly thickened. Fold in whipped topping. Pour into 6-cup mold. Chill until set but not firm.

Add remaining measured liquid to remaining gelatin. Chill until thickened; fold in sliced berries. Spoon over creamy layer in mold. Chill until firm, about 4 hours. Unmold. Garnish with reserved berries.

*Substitution: Use ½ teaspoon brandy extract and 3 tablespoons orange juice for the brandy and orange liqueur.

Buffet Slaw

Makes about 6 cups or 12 servings

2 cans (8¼ ounces each) crushed pineapple in juice

2 packages (4-serving size) or 1 package (8-serving size)
   JELL-O® Brand Lemon Flavor Gelatin

1½ cups boiling water

  Ice cubes

3 tablespoons vinegar

½ teaspoon celery salt

1 cup each finely shredded green and red cabbage

¼ cup chopped parsley

1 tablespoon finely chopped onion

Drain pineapple, reserving juice. Add water to juice to make 1 cup; set aside. Completely dissolve gelatin in boiling water. Combine measured liquid and ice cubes to make 2½ cups. Add to gelatin with vinegar and celery salt, stirring until slightly thickened. Remove any unmelted ice. Chill until thickened, about 10 minutes. Fold in pineapple, cabbage, parsley and onion. Pour into 8-cup bowl. Chill until set, about 3 hours. Garnish with cabbage leaves, parsley and onion rings, if desired.

Neapolitan Vegetable Mold

Makes 5½ cups or 10 servings

2 packages (4-serving size) or 1 package (8-serving size)
   JELL-O® Brand Lemon Flavor Gelatin

1 teaspoon salt

2 cups boiling water

1½ cups cold water

3 tablespoons vinegar

1½ cups shredded carrots

½ cup mayonnaise

1 cup finely chopped cabbage

1½ cups finely chopped spinach

1 teaspoon grated onion

CONTINUED

Dissolve gelatin and salt in boiling water. Add cold water and vinegar. Measure 1⅓ cups of the gelatin into bowl. Place bowl in larger bowl of ice and water; stir until slightly thickened. Stir in carrots and pour into 6-cup ring mold or 9×5-inch loaf pan. Chill until set but not firm.

Measure 1 cup of the remaining gelatin; blend in mayonnaise. Chill over ice until thickened. Stir in cabbage; spoon over carrot layer in mold. Chill.

Chill remaining gelatin over ice until slightly thickened. Add spinach and onion. Spoon over mayonnaise layer in mold. Chill until firm, about 3 hours. Unmold. Garnish with chicory and carrot curls, if desired.

LAYERED STRAWBERRY-CRACKER DESSERT

Makes 9 servings

2 packages (4-serving size) or 1 package (8-serving size)
   JELL-O® Brand Strawberry Flavor Gelatin
2 cups boiling water
1 cup cold water
1 pint strawberries
2 tablespoons sugar (optional)
3½ cups (8 ounces) COOL WHIP® Non-Dairy Whipped
   Topping, thawed
18 graham cracker squares

Dissolve gelatin in boiling water. Add cold water. Chill until slightly thickened. Meanwhile, slice strawberries, reserving a few whole berries for garnish, if desired. Sprinkle sliced berries with sugar. Fold whipped topping into gelatin, blending well; fold in sliced berries.

Place 9 graham cracker squares in bottom of 9-inch square pan. Spread half of the gelatin mixture over crackers. Repeat layers. Chill until firm, about 3 hours. Cut into squares. Garnish with reserved strawberries and additional whipped topping, if desired.

—■—

CHOCOLATE CHEESECAKE

Makes 12 servings

1 package (4-serving size) JELL-O® Chocolate or Chocolate
 Fudge Flavor Pudding and Pie Filling

¾ cup sugar

1 cup milk

2 squares BAKER'S® Unsweetened Chocolate, coarsely
 chopped

2 teaspoons vanilla

3 packages (8 ounces each) cream cheese, softened

3 eggs, separated

Microwave:* Combine pudding mix, sugar and milk in 1½-quart micro-wave-safe bowl; blend well. Add chocolate. Cook at HIGH 3 minutes. Stir well and cook 2 minutes longer, until mixture comes to a full boil. Add vanilla; set aside.

With electric mixer at medium speed, beat cream cheese in large bowl until smooth. Beat in egg yolks; then add reserved pudding. Place egg whites in small narrow bowl. With clean beaters and electric mixer at high speed, beat until stiff peaks form. Gently fold in small amount of cheese mixture. Fold egg white mixture into remaining cheese mixture, blending well. Pour into 12×7½-inch microwave-safe dish, lightly greased on bottom only.

Place dish on inverted microwave-safe pie plate. Cook at HIGH 10 to 12 minutes, rotating dish several times, until evenly puffed across top. Place on flat heatproof surface; cool to room temperature. Cut into squares. Store in refrigerator.

*Ovens vary. Cooking time is approximate.

FOR THE HOLIDAYS

Festive salads and desserts that reflect the
spirit of the season. Brighten your holiday table
with these exciting new ways to use
traditional flavors. What better way to celebrate when
family and friends gather!

Peppermint Dessert

— ■ —

PEPPERMINT DESSERT

Makes 3¼ cups or 6 or 7 servings

6 to 8 round peppermint candies*
  ¾ cup water
  1 package (4-serving size) JELL-O® Brand Gelatin, any red
     flavor
  ½ cup cold water
    Ice cubes
1¾ cups thawed COOL WHIP® Non-Dairy Whipped Topping

Break candies in half. Combine candies and the ¾ cup water in small saucepan. Bring to a boil over medium-high heat, stirring until candies are melted. Completely dissolve gelatin in boiling liquid. Combine the ½ cup cold water and ice cubes to make 1¼ cups. Add to gelatin, stirring until slightly thickened. Remove any unmelted ice. Pour 1½ cups of the gelatin into serving bowl or individual dessert dishes. Chill until set but not firm, about 5 to 10 minutes.

Spread ¾ cup of the whipped topping over gelatin. Blend remaining whipped topping into remaining gelatin. Spoon over whipped topping in bowl. Chill about 1 hour. Garnish with additional whipped topping and peppermint candies.

*Substitution: Use 2 candy canes (7-inch), broken into 1-inch pieces.

CRANBERRY-LEMON PIE

Makes one 9-inch pie

  1 package (4-serving size) JELL-O® Brand Lemon Flavor
     Gelatin
  ¾ cup boiling water
  1 can (16 ounces) whole berry cranberry sauce
1¾ cups thawed COOL WHIP® Non-Dairy Whipped Topping
  1 baked 9-inch pie shell, cooled

Dissolve gelatin in boiling water. Add cranberry sauce; mix well. Chill until slightly thickened. Fold in whipped topping. Spoon into pie shell. Chill until set, about 2 hours. Garnish with additional whipped topping, lemon slices or fresh cranberries, if desired.

— ■ —

PUDDING PECAN PIE

Makes one 8-inch pie

1 package (4-serving size) JELL-O® Vanilla or
    Butterscotch Flavor Instant Pudding and Pie Filling*
1 cup light or dark corn syrup
¾ cup evaporated milk
1 egg, slightly beaten
1 cup chopped pecans**
1 unbaked 8-inch pie shell

Combine pie filling mix with corn syrup in medium bowl. With electric mixer at low speed, blend. Gradually add evaporated milk and egg; blend well. Stir in nuts; pour into pie shell. Bake in preheated 375° oven until top is firm and just begins to crack, 45 to 50 minutes. Cool on wire rack at least 3 hours before serving. Garnish with whipped topping and additional pecans, if desired.

*Substitution: Use butter pecan flavor instant pudding and pie filling, reducing pecans to ½ cup.

**Substitution: Use ½ cup chopped pecans and ½ cup BAKER'S® ANGEL FLAKE® Coconut.

FROZEN PUMPKIN SQUARES

Makes 9 servings

1¼ cups fine gingersnap crumbs
¼ cup finely chopped walnuts
¼ cup butter or margarine
1 cup cold milk
1 cup canned solid-pack pumpkin
1 teaspoon pumpkin pie spice*
1 package (6-serving size) JELL-O® Vanilla Flavor Instant
    Pudding and Pie Filling
3½ cups (8 ounces) COOL WHIP® Non-Dairy Whipped
    Topping, thawed

CONTINUED

Combine crumbs, nuts and butter; mix well. Press firmly on bottom of 8-inch square pan. Chill for at least 15 minutes. Combine cold milk, pumpkin and spice in bowl. Add pudding mix. With electric mixer at low speed, beat until well blended, 1 to 2 minutes. Fold in 2¼ cups of the whipped topping. Spoon over crumb crust in pan. Freeze until firm, about 4 hours.

Let stand at room temperature about 10 minutes. Cut into squares; garnish with remaining whipped topping and additional nuts, if desired. Store any leftover dessert in freezer.

*Substitution: Use ½ teaspoon cinnamon and ¼ teaspoon each ginger and nutmeg.

SPICY CRANBERRY-ORANGE MOLD

Makes about 6 cups or 12 servings

1½ cups ground fresh cranberries*

½ cup sugar*

2 packages (4-serving size) or 1 package (8-serving size)
    JELL-O® Brand Orange or Lemon Flavor Gelatin

¼ teaspoon salt

2 cups boiling water

1½ cups cold water*

1 tablespoon lemon juice

¼ teaspoon cinnamon

⅛ teaspoon cloves

1 orange, sectioned and diced

½ cup chopped walnuts, almonds or celery

Combine cranberries and sugar; set aside. Dissolve gelatin and salt in boiling water. Add cold water, lemon juice, cinnamon and cloves. Chill until thickened. Fold in cranberries, orange and nuts. Spoon into 6-cup ring mold. Chill until firm, about 4 hours. Unmold. Garnish with salad greens, if desired.

*Substitution: Use 1 can (16 ounces) whole berry cranberry sauce, omitting sugar and reducing cold water to 1 cup.

CHUTNEY RELISH

Makes about 2 cups or 6 relish servings

    6 whole cloves
1¾ cups water
    1 package (4-serving size) JELL-O® Brand Apricot or
       Lemon Flavor Gelatin
½ teaspoon salt
½ cup chutney, drained and finely chopped*
    1 teaspoon prepared horseradish

Combine cloves and 1 cup of the water in small saucepan. Bring to a boil over high heat; boil 3 minutes. Remove and discard cloves. Dissolve gelatin and salt in hot liquid. Pour into bowl. Add remaining water. Chill until thickened. Fold in chutney and horseradish. Chill until firm, about 3 hours. Spoon into serving bowl.

*Substitution: Use 1 cup India relish.

— ■ —

MOLDED CHEESE

Makes 5½ cups or 11 servings

2 packages (4-serving size) or 1 package (8-serving size)
   JELL-O® Brand Orange or Lemon Flavor Gelatin
1½ cups boiling water
½ pound (2½ cups) finely grated sharp Cheddar cheese
1 package (8 ounces) cream cheese, softened
1 cup (½ pint) sour cream
½ cup chopped scallions
¼ cup chopped parsley
3 tablespoons prepared horseradish
1 tablespoon Worcestershire sauce

Dissolve gelatin in boiling water. Combine remaining ingredients in large bowl; with electric mixer at medium speed, beat until well blended. Gradually blend into gelatin. Pour into 6-cup mold. Chill until firm, about 3 hours. Unmold. Garnish with fresh fruit or vegetables, if desired. Serve as an appetizer with assorted crackers.

LAYERED PARTY CRANBERRY SALAD

Makes 6¾ cups or 12 servings

 2 packages (4-serving size) or 1 package (8-serving size)
   JELL-O® Brand Raspberry Flavor Gelatin
 3 cups boiling water
¾ cup cold water
½ cup port wine
 1 cup whole berry cranberry sauce
½ cup chopped apple
½ cup chopped walnuts
 1 package (4-serving size) JELL-O® Brand Lemon Flavor
   Gelatin
½ cup mayonnaise
1¾ cups thawed COOL WHIP® Non-Dairy Whipped Topping

Dissolve 1 package of the raspberry flavor gelatin in 1 cup of the boiling water. Add ¼ cup of the cold water and ¼ cup of the wine; chill until slightly thickened. Fold in cranberry sauce, apple and nuts. Pour into 2-quart serving bowl. Chill until set but not firm.

Dissolve lemon flavor gelatin in 1 cup of the boiling water. Chill until slightly thickened; then blend in mayonnaise and whipped topping. Pour over gelatin in bowl. Chill until set but not firm.

Meanwhile, dissolve remaining raspberry flavor gelatin in remaining boiling water. Add remaining cold water and wine. Chill until slightly thickened. Pour over lemon layer in bowl. Chill until firm, about 3 hours. Garnish with sugared green grapes, if desired.

RUM-NUT PUDDING CAKE

Makes one 10-inch cake

1 cup chopped pecans or walnuts
1 package (2-layer size) yellow cake mix*
1 package (4-serving size) JELL-O® Vanilla or Butter Pecan
  Flavor Instant Pudding and Pie Filling
4 eggs
¾ cup water*
¼ cup vegetable oil
⅔ cup dark rum
1 cup sugar
½ cup butter or margarine

Sprinkle nuts evenly in bottom of greased and floured 10-inch tube or fluted tube pan. Combine cake mix, pudding mix, eggs, ½ cup of the water, the oil and ⅓ cup of the rum in large bowl. With electric mixer at low speed, blend just to moisten, scraping sides of bowl often. Then beat at medium speed for 4 minutes. Pour batter into pan. Bake in preheated 325° oven for about 1 hour or until cake tester inserted in center comes out clean and cake begins to pull away from sides of pan. Do not underbake. Cool in pan on wire rack 15 minutes.

Meanwhile, combine sugar, butter and remaining ¼ cup water in small saucepan. Cook and stir over medium-high heat until mixture comes to a boil; boil 5 minutes, stirring constantly. Stir in remaining rum and bring just to a boil.

Invert cake onto serving plate and prick with cake tester or wooden pick. Carefully spoon warm syrup over warm cake. Garnish with whipped topping and pecans, if desired.

*Substitution: Use pudding-included cake mix, reducing water in batter to ¼ cup.

Rum-Nut Pudding Cake ▶

CREAMY PUMPKIN DESSERT

Makes about 7 cups or 14 servings

2 packages (4-serving size) or 1 package (8-serving size)
   JELL-O® Brand Lemon Flavor Gelatin

1½ cups boiling water

1 package (8 ounces) cream cheese, softened

1 can (29 ounces) solid-pack pumpkin

2¼ teaspoons cinnamon

½ teaspoon nutmeg

½ teaspoon ginger

3 cups thawed COOL WHIP® Non-Dairy Whipped Topping

1 cup chopped pecans

2 tablespoons brown sugar

CONTINUED

196

Dissolve gelatin in boiling water. With electric mixer at medium speed, beat cream cheese until smooth. Blend in pumpkin, 2 teaspoons of the cinnamon, the nutmeg, ginger and gelatin. Chill until thickened. Fold in whipped topping. Pour half of the pumpkin mixture into 8-cup serving bowl. Combine nuts, brown sugar and remaining cinnamon; sprinkle over pumpkin mixture in bowl. Top with remaining pumpkin mixture. Chill until set, about 3 hours. Garnish with additional whipped topping and pecan halves, if desired.

CREAMY APPLE-PECAN PIE

Makes one 9-inch pie

- 1 can (20 to 21 ounces) apple, cherry, blueberry or peach pie filling
- 2 tablespoons brown sugar
- ¼ teaspoon cinnamon
- ¼ cup chopped pecans
- 1 baked 9-inch pie shell or prepared graham cracker crumb crust, cooled
- ½ cup cold milk
- ½ cup half and half or light cream
- 1 package (4-serving size) JELL-O® Vanilla Flavor Instant Pudding and Pie Filling
- 1½ cups thawed COOL WHIP® Non-Dairy Whipped Topping

Combine apple pie filling, brown sugar and cinnamon; add nuts. Spread half of the apple mixture in pie shell; chill remaining apple mixture.

Pour cold milk and half and half into bowl. Add pie filling mix. With electric mixer at low speed, beat until well blended, 1 to 2 minutes. Fold in whipped topping. Spoon over apple mixture in pie shell. Freeze 1 hour or chill 3 hours before serving. Garnish with remaining apple mixture and additional whipped topping, if desired.

HOLIDAY PARFAIT

Makes 6 cups or 12 servings

　1 can (11 ounces) mandarin orange sections
1½ cups fresh cranberries
　¼ cup sugar
　1 package (4-serving size) JELL-O® Brand Orange Flavor
　　　Gelatin
　½ cup cold water
　　　Ice cubes
1¼ cups cold milk
　1 package (4-serving size) JELL-O® Vanilla or
　　　Butterscotch Flavor Instant Pudding and Pie Filling
　1 cup canned solid-pack pumpkin
　1 cup thawed COOL WHIP® Non-Dairy Whipped Topping
　½ teaspoon each cinnamon, ginger and nutmeg
　　　or 1½ teaspoons pumpkin pie spice

Drain orange sections, reserving liquid. Add water to reserved liquid to make ¾ cup; pour into medium saucepan. Add cranberries. Cook over medium heat until cranberries are soft, about 5 to 10 minutes, stirring frequently. Add sugar and gelatin; stir until completely dissolved. Remove saucepan from heat. Combine cold water and ice cubes to make 1¼ cups. Add to gelatin mixture, stirring until ice is melted. Reserve a few orange sections for garnish. Stir remaining sections into gelatin mixture. Pour into individual parfait glasses, filling each about half full. Chill until set, about 1 hour.

Pour cold milk into bowl. Add pudding mix. With electric mixer at low speed, beat until well blended, 1 to 2 minutes. Blend in pumpkin, whipped topping and spices. Spoon over gelatin in glasses. Chill. Garnish with additional whipped topping, reserved orange sections and chopped pecans, if desired.

PUMPKIN MOUSSE

Makes 3¼ cups or 6 servings

1¼ cups cold milk

1 cup canned solid-pack pumpkin

1 teaspoon grated orange rind (optional)

¼ teaspoon each cinnamon, nutmeg and ginger
or ¾ teaspoon pumpkin pie spice

1 package (4-serving size) JELL-O® Vanilla or
Butterscotch Flavor Instant Pudding and Pie Filling
Mix

1 cup thawed COOL WHIP® Non-Dairy Whipped Topping

¼ cup chopped pecans (optional)

Combine cold milk, pumpkin, orange rind and spices in bowl. Add pudding mix. With electric mixer at low speed, beat until well blended, 1 to 2 minutes. Fold in whipped topping and nuts. Spoon into individual dessert glasses. Chill. Garnish with additional whipped topping and nuts, if desired.

CRANBERRY PUDDING CAKE WITH SAUCE

Makes two 9×5-inch loaves

- 1 package (2-layer size) yellow cake mix*
- 1 package (4-serving size) JELL-O® Lemon Flavor Instant Pudding and Pie Filling
- 4 eggs
- 1 cup (½ pint) sour cream*
- ¼ cup vegetable oil
- ½ cup chopped nuts
- 1 can (16 ounces) whole berry cranberry sauce or jellied cranberry sauce cut in small cubes
- 1 package (4-serving size) JELL-O® Lemon Flavor Pudding and Pie Filling
- ½ cup sugar
- ¼ teaspoon salt
- 1 tablespoon butter or margarine

CONTINUED

Combine cake mix, instant pudding mix, eggs, sour cream, oil and nuts in large bowl. With electric mixer at low speed, blend just to moisten, scraping sides of bowl often. Then beat at medium speed for 4 minutes. Fold in half of the cranberry sauce. Pour batter into 2 greased and floured 9×5-inch loaf pans. Bake in preheated 350° oven for 50 to 55 minutes or until cake tester inserted in center of cake comes out clean and cake begins to pull away from sides of pan. Do not underbake. Cool in pans on wire rack 15 minutes. Remove from pans and finish cooling on wire rack.

Add water to remaining cranberry sauce to make 2½ cups. Combine pudding mix, sugar, salt and measured liquid in medium saucepan. Cook and stir over medium heat until mixture comes to a full boil and is thickened. Remove from heat. Stir in butter. Serve warm over cake.

*Substitution: Use pudding-included cake mix, decreasing sour cream to ¾ cup.

EGGNOG PIE

Makes one 9-inch pie

1 cup cold dairy or canned eggnog
1 package (6-serving size) JELL-O® Vanilla Flavor Instant Pudding and Pie Filling
1 tablespoon rum or ¼ teaspoon rum extract
¼ teaspoon nutmeg
3½ cups (8 ounces) COOL WHIP® Non-Dairy Whipped Topping, thawed
1 prepared 8- to 9-inch graham cracker crumb crust, cooled

Pour cold eggnog into bowl. Add pie filling mix, rum and nutmeg. With electric mixer at low speed, beat until blended, about 1 minute. Let stand 5 minutes. Fold in 2 cups of the whipped topping. Spoon into pie crust. Chill until firm, about 2 hours. Garnish with remaining whipped topping. Sprinkle with additional nutmeg, if desired.

CHRISTMAS RIBBON

Makes about 6 cups or 12 servings

> 2 packages (4-serving size) or 1 package (8-serving size)
>   JELL-O® Brand Strawberry Flavor Gelatin
> 5 cups boiling water
> ⅔ cup sour cream or vanilla yogurt
> 2 packages (4-serving size) or 1 package (8-serving size)
>   JELL-O® Brand Lime Flavor Gelatin

Dissolve strawberry flavor gelatin in 2½ cups of the boiling water. Pour 1½ cups of the strawberry flavor gelatin into 6-cup ring mold. Chill until set but not firm, about 30 minutes. Chill remaining strawberry flavor gelatin in bowl until slightly thickened. Gradually blend in ⅓ cup of the sour cream. Spoon over gelatin in mold. Chill until set but not firm, about 15 minutes.

Dissolve lime flavor gelatin in remaining boiling water. Chill until slightly thickened. Pour 1½ cups of the lime flavor gelatin over creamy layer in mold. Chill until set but not firm, about 15 minutes. Chill remaining lime flavor gelatin in bowl until slightly thickened. Gradually blend in remaining sour cream. Spoon over gelatin in mold. Chill about 2 hours. Unmold.

HOLIDAY WALDORF SALAD

Makes about 7 cups or 14 servings

> 2 packages (4-serving size) or 1 package (8-serving size)
>   JELL-O® Brand Strawberry Flavor Gelatin
> 1½ cups boiling water
> 1 tablespoon lemon juice
> 1 cup cold water
>   Ice cubes
> 1 medium red apple, diced
> ½ cup halved seedless grapes
> ½ cup thinly sliced celery
> ½ cup chopped walnuts
> 1 cup mayonnaise

CONTINUED

Completely dissolve gelatin in boiling water; add lemon juice. Combine cold water and ice cubes to make 2½ cups. Add to gelatin, stirring until slightly thickened. Remove any unmelted ice. Chill until thickened, about 10 minutes. Fold in apple, grapes, celery and nuts. Measure 1 cup of the gelatin and set aside. Pour remaining gelatin into 8-cup bowl. Chill until set but not firm.

Blend mayonnaise into measured gelatin. Spoon over fruited layer in bowl. Chill until set, about 3 hours. Garnish with fresh fruit and crisp greens, if desired.

FLUFFY NESSELRODE PIE

Makes one 9-inch pie

Quick Sweet Chocolate Coconut Crust (recipe follows)
1 package (8 ounces) cream cheese, softened
1 cup cold milk
2 tablespoons light rum or 1 teaspoon rum extract
1 package (4-serving size) JELL-O® Vanilla Flavor Instant
    Pudding and Pie Filling
½ cup mixed candied fruit, finely chopped
3 cups thawed COOL WHIP® Non-Dairy Whipped Topping

Prepare Quick Sweet Chocolate Coconut Crust; set aside. With electric mixer at low speed, beat cream cheese until very soft. Gradually add ½ cup of the milk, beating until smooth. Add remaining milk, the rum and pie filling mix; beat at low speed until blended, 1 minute. Fold in fruit and whipped topping. Spoon into pie crust. Chill until firm, about 4 hours. Garnish with additional whipped topping and chocolate curls, if desired.

Quick Sweet Chocolate Coconut Crust: Combine 1 package (4 ounces) BAKER'S® GERMAN'S® Sweet Chocolate and 2 tablespoons butter or margarine in medium saucepan. Heat over low heat until chocolate is melted, stirring constantly. Remove from heat. Stir in 2 cups BAKER'S® ANGEL FLAKE® Coconut; mix well. Press on bottom and sides of 9-inch pie plate. Chill until firm, about 4 hours.

CREAMY HOLIDAY MOLD

Makes about 5 cups or 10 servings

1 package (4-serving size) JELL-O® Brand Lemon Flavor
    Gelatin

1 package (4-serving size) JELL-O® Vanilla Flavor Pudding
    and Pie Filling

2 cups water

½ teaspoon vanilla

¼ teaspoon rum extract (optional)

⅛ teaspoon nutmeg

3 cups thawed COOL WHIP® Non-Dairy Whipped Topping

Combine gelatin, pudding mix and water in medium saucepan; blend well. Cook and stir over medium heat until mixture comes to a full boil. Remove from heat. Chill until thickened. Blend in vanilla, rum extract and nutmeg. Fold in whipped topping. Pour into 5- or 6-cup mold. Chill until firm, about 3 hours. Unmold. Garnish with additional whipped topping and stemmed maraschino cherries, if desired.

CRANBERRY PINEAPPLE RELISH

Makes about 6½ cups or 12 servings

1 can (20 ounces) pineapple chunks in syrup

2 packages (4-serving size) or 1 package (8-serving size)
    JELL-O® Brand Raspberry Flavor Gelatin

1½ cups boiling water

    Ice cubes

2½ cups fresh cranberries, chopped

½ cup chopped pecans

Drain pineapple, reserving syrup. Add water to syrup to make 1 cup. Completely dissolve gelatin in boiling water. Combine measured liquid and ice cubes to make 2½ cups. Add to gelatin, stirring until slightly thickened. Remove any unmelted ice. Chill until thickened, about 10 minutes. Fold in pineapple, cranberries and nuts. Pour into 8-cup bowl. Chill until set, about 3 hours. Garnish with endive leaves and sugared cranberries, if desired.

— ◼ —

LAYERED PRALINE PIE

Makes one 9-inch pie

⅓ cup butter or margarine
⅓ cup packed brown sugar
½ cup chopped pecans
1 lightly baked 9-inch pie shell*
1 package (6-serving size) JELL-O® Vanilla Flavor Pudding and Pie Filling**
2½ cups milk
1¾ cups thawed COOL WHIP® Non-Dairy Whipped Topping

Combine butter, brown sugar and nuts in medium saucepan. Heat over medium heat until butter and sugar are melted. Spread in bottom of pie shell. Bake in preheated 450° oven for 5 minutes or until bubbly. Cool on wire rack.

Combine pie filling mix and milk in another medium saucepan. Cook and stir over medium heat until mixture comes to a full boil. Pie filling thickens as it cools. Cool 5 minutes, stirring twice. Measure 1 cup; cover with plastic wrap and chill thoroughly. Pour remaining pie filling into pie shell; chill. Blend 1⅓ cups of the whipped topping into measured chilled pie filling. Spoon into pie shell; chill at least 3 hours. Garnish with remaining whipped topping.

*Decrease recommended baking time by 5 minutes.

**Substitution: Use 2 packages (4-serving size) JELL-O® Vanilla Flavor Pudding and Pie Filling, increasing milk to 3½ cups.

GELATIN POKE LAYER CAKE

Makes one 8- or 9-inch cake

2 baked 8- or 9-inch white cake layers, cooled
2 packages (4-serving size) or 1 package (8-serving size) JELL-O® Brand Gelatin, any flavor
2 cups boiling water
3½ cups (8 ounces) COOL WHIP® Non-Dairy Whipped Topping, thawed

CONTINUED

— ◼ —

Place cake layers, top-side up, in 2 clean 8- or 9-inch cake pans. Prick each cake with utility fork at ½-inch intervals. Dissolve gelatin in boiling water. Carefully spoon over cake layers. Chill 3 to 4 hours. Dip 1 cake pan in warm water for 10 seconds; then unmold onto serving plate. Top with about 1 cup of the whipped topping. Unmold second cake layer and carefully place on first layer. Frost top and sides with remaining whipped topping. Chill. Garnish as desired.

Holly Poke Layer Cake: Prepare Gelatin Poke Layer Cake as directed, using 1 package (4-serving size) each raspberry and lime flavor gelatin. Dissolve each flavor gelatin separately in 1 cup boiling water. Pour raspberry flavor gelatin over 1 of the cake layers. Pour lime flavor gelatin over remaining cake layer. Garnish with Gumdrop Holly Leaves (recipe follows) and gumdrop berries, if desired.

Gumdrop Holly Leaves: Sprinkle pastry board with sugar or JELL-O® Brand Lime Flavor Gelatin. Flatten green gumdrops with rolling pin until about ¹⁄₁₆ inch thick, turning frequently to coat with sugar. Cut flattened gumdrops into holly leaf shapes. Let leaves stand overnight uncovered to dry. Use wooden picks, if desired, to attach leaves to cake.

Holly Poke Layer Cake

INSTANT PUMPKIN PIE

Makes one 8-inch pie

⅔ cup cold milk

1 package (4-serving size) JELL-O® Vanilla or
   Butterscotch Flavor Instant Pudding and Pie Filling

1 cup canned solid-pack pumpkin

¼ teaspoon each cinnamon, nutmeg and ginger
   or ¾ teaspoon pumpkin pie spice

¼ cup chopped pecans (optional)

1¾ cups thawed COOL WHIP® Non-Dairy Whipped Topping

1 baked 8-inch pie shell or prepared graham cracker crumb
   crust, cooled

Pour cold milk into bowl. Add pie filling mix. With electric mixer at low speed, beat just until blended, about 30 seconds. Blend in pumpkin, spices, nuts and 1 cup of the whipped topping. Spoon into pie shell. Chill about 2 hours. Garnish with remaining whipped topping and orange slices, if desired.

Note: Recipe may be doubled, using 1 can (16 ounces) solid-pack pumpkin and 9-inch pie shell.

CRANBERRY PUDDING ICE CREAM PIE

Makes one 9-inch pie

1 can (8 ounces) jellied cranberry sauce

1 baked 9-inch pie shell, cooled

1 cup cold milk

1 cup (½ pint) vanilla ice cream, softened

1 package (4-serving size) JELL-O® Vanilla Flavor Instant
   Pudding and Pie Filling

Remove cranberry sauce from can in one piece; cut into thin slices and arrange on bottom of pie shell. Combine milk and ice cream in medium bowl until thoroughly blended. Add pie filling mix. With electric mixer at low speed, beat until blended, about 1 minute. Pour immediately into pie shell. Chill about 1 hour. Garnish with whipped topping and whole berry cranberry sauce, if desired.

— ■ —

CREAMY LEMON PIE

Makes one 8-inch pie

¾ cup cold milk

¾ cup cold light cream or half and half

1 package (4-serving size) JELL-O® Lemon Flavor Instant
   Pudding and Pie Filling

¼ teaspoon vanilla

⅛ teaspoon nutmeg

1 prepared 8-inch graham cracker crumb crust or baked
   pie shell, cooled

1¾ cups thawed COOL WHIP® Non-Dairy Whipped Topping

Pour cold milk and light cream into bowl. Add pie filling mix, vanilla and nutmeg. With electric mixer at low speed, beat until blended, about 1 minute. Quickly measure 1¼ cups of the pie filling; pour into pie crust. Chill.

Measure 1 cup of the whipped topping and blend into remaining pie filling mixture. Spread over pie filling in pie crust. Chill about 1 hour. Garnish with remaining whipped topping, strawberry halves and mint leaves, if desired.

Clockwise from top: Instant Pumpkin Pie, Cranberry Pudding Ice Cream Pie, Creamy Lemon Pie

FROZEN FRUITCAKE

Makes one 8 × 4-inch loaf

½ cup golden raisins

¼ cup rum*

1 package (4-serving size) JELL-O® Vanilla Flavor Pudding
    and Pie Filling**

2 cups milk

1 teaspoon vanilla

1⅓ cups (about) BAKER'S® ANGEL FLAKE® Coconut

    Maraschino cherries, halved

    Pecan halves

½ cup coarsely chopped pecans

½ cup sliced pitted dates

¾ cup dry macaroon or coconut cookie crumbs

1¾ cups thawed COOL WHIP® Non-Dairy Whipped Topping

Plump raisins in rum in small bowl; set aside. Combine pudding mix and milk in medium saucepan; blend well. Cook and stir over medium heat until mixture comes to a full boil. Stir in vanilla and coconut. Cover with plastic wrap; chill.

Arrange cherry and pecan halves in design on bottom of lightly greased 8×4-inch loaf pan. Fold raisins, chopped nuts, dates and crumbs into chilled pudding. Fold in 1½ cups of the whipped topping. Carefully spoon mixture into pan. Freeze until firm, about 8 hours. Unmold. Garnish with remaining whipped topping.

*Substitution: Use ¼ cup water and 1 teaspoon rum extract.

**Substitution: Use 1 package (4-serving size) JELL-O® Vanilla Flavor Instant Pudding and Pie Filling, preparing according to package directions.

INDEX

INDEX

—■—

—■—

INDEX

—■—

—■—

INDEX

— ■ —

— ■ —

INDEX

— ◼ —

— ◼ —

INDEX

— ■ —

— ■ —